F. R. LEAVIS

CRITICS OF THE TWENTIETH CENTURY
Edited by Christopher Norris, University of Wales
Institute of Science and Technology

F. R. LEAVIS

MICHAEL BELL

ROUTLEDGE
London and New York

First published in 1988 by
Routledge
11 New Fetter Lane, London EC4P 4EE

Published in the USA by
Routledge
in association with Routledge, Chapman and Hall, Inc.
29 West 35th Street, New York NY 10001

Printed and bound in Great Britain by
Biddles Ltd, Guildford and King's Lynn

Typeset by Pat and Anne Murphy, Highcliffe-on-Sea, Dorset

British Library Cataloguing in Publication Data

Bell, Michael, *1941 –*
   F. R. Leavis.
   1. Literature. Criticism. Leavis, F. R.
   (Frank Raymond), 1895 – 1978. Critical
   studies.
   I. Title
   801'.95'0924

   ISBN 0-415-00897-2
   ISBN 0-415-00898-0 Pbk

Library of Congress Cataloging-in-Publication Data

Bell, Michael, 1941 –
   F. R. Leavis / Michael Bell.
   p. cm. — (Critics of the twentieth century)
   Bibliography: p.
   ISBN 0 415 00897 2.   ISBN 0 415 00898 0 (pbk.)
   1. Leavis, F. R. (Frank Raymond), 1895 –   .
   2. Criticism — Great Britain — History — 20th century.
   3. English literature — History and criticism.
   I. Title. II. Series.
   PR29.L4B45 1988
   801'.95'0924 – dc 19

Contents

Editor's Foreword

F. R. Leavis was undoubtedly the single most influential figure in twentieth-century English literary criticism. Indeed, it is no exaggeration to say that 'English' as a modern university subject was shaped very largely by Leavis's example, his writings and their influence on successive generations of teachers and students. As a young lecturer at Cambridge, Leavis set out to transform English Studies from a gentleman–amateur pursuit into a discipline of trained critical awareness and high moral vocation. From T. S. Eliot he took the idea of 'tradition' as a highly selective canon of texts whose qualities could only be perceived and preserved through the utmost efforts of applied critical intelligence. From I. A. Richards he derived certain crucial ideas about the nature and specific complexity of poetic language, though rejecting what he saw as the narrowly scientistic basis of Richards's work. And one could instance William Empson's pioneering *Seven types of ambiguity* (1930) — published during Leavis's formative years — as having clearly left its mark on his close-reading approach to poetry and his sense of the new insights offered by meticulous verbal analysis. In short, one could claim that there was, after all, nothing very 'original' about Leavis, save only his extreme and single-minded belief in the absolute centrality of 'English' as a discipline of thought. But it can equally be argued that this was indeed the nature of Leavis's original contribution. Somehow his conviction moved out beyond its base in the Cambridge English Faculty to define what amounted to a whole new discourse on and around the henceforth controversial subject of English Studies.

Some measure of this singular pervasive presence may be taken from the efforts of recent commentators to diagnose the sources of Leavis's potent appeal by placing it in relation to a certain *ideology* of English cultural values.[1] Thus his work can be seen as a substitute for other kinds of thinking, themselves largely absent or underdeveloped in the mainstream of British intellectual life. In place of any Marxist or other form of socio-political critique, Leavis held out the idea of *English* — of a training for maturity in literary studies — as the one hope of renewal and growth in an otherwise irredeemable 'mass-civilisation'. This idea he inherited from thinkers like Coleridge and Matthew Arnold, proponents of a

cultural criticism that would save humankind from the disinte-
grating forces of modern secular society by conserving those
imaginative values and energies that transcended mere instrumental reason. Hence Leavis's well-known aversion to 'theory', his
quarrel with those (like René Wellek) who wanted him to be more
explicit about the precepts and principles underlying his work.[2]
'Theory' for Leavis was the active antithesis of everything that
good, responsible criticism ought to be. Theory was a matter of
abstract ideas, of lifeless generalities which nowhere engaged with
the vital, responsive, intuitive nature of authentic critical insight.
Toward the end of his life Leavis found something of interest and
value in the work of two philosophers (Michael Polanyi and
Marjorie Grene) who had themselves raised questions about the
limits of analysis or conceptual knowledge.[3] Particularly useful,
Leavis thought, was Polanyi's notion of 'tacit understanding' as
the largely inexplicit (and hence untheorisable) basis of all human
knowledge. But his attitude remained pretty much unaltered, as
witness the title of a posthumous volume of Leavis's essays: *The
critic as anti-philosopher*.

Recent commentators have had a good deal to say about
Leavis's antipathy to theory. Some — notably Tom Nairn and
Perry Anderson[4] — have seen it as an ideological reflex, a rear-
guard defence of humanistic values that claim to transcend all class
affiliations but in fact belong firmly to a late, beleaguered phase of
petty-bourgeois cultural politics. Leavis's refusal to theorise his
position would then represent a retreat in the face of mounting
historical pressures, a desire at all costs to save criticism from
acknowledging its own political interests. This resistance to theory
among British intellectuals goes back to the period of intense ideological debate sparked off by the French Revolution. From Burke
and the later Coleridge to Arnold, Eliot and Leavis, it is a form of
conservative reaction which attempts to drive a wedge between
'culture' and 'society' by treating the one as a separate sphere of
absolute, timeless values and the other as witness of a secular
decline which criticism can only deplore from its standpoint of elite
minority culture. Of course not all these thinkers were 'against'
theory in an absolute or general sense. Coleridge indeed did more
than anyone to acquaint British readers with Kantian critical
philosophy and its bearings on literary criticism. But in his later
writings — disenchanted with events in the wake of the French
Revolution — Coleridge falls back on a distinctly Burkean way of
thinking about history, politics and culture. It is the good fortune

of the British not to be obsessed, like the French, with theoretical notions of justice, equality and truth. Theirs is the opposite way, a decent regard for inherited values and a sense of the social good as consisting in a long-term 'organic' community of spirit beyond mere conflicts of material class-interest. Hence the transition in Coleridge's thought from an organicist aesthetics, based on ideas of unity-in-multiplicity, to the view of social order as a mystical estate likewise transcending sectarian divisions. It is a stance taken up by Matthew Arnold in his plea that the 'philistine' Victorian middle classes should set themselves to read, think and feel more deeply and thus acquire the kind of *cultural* leadership — the hegemonic power — to overcome threatening social disorders by embodying a spirit of new-found national identity. By Eliot's time, in his *Notes towards the definition of culture*, this idea has reached the end of its historical tether and become a last-ditch obscurantist appeal to some divinely-sanctioned order of social inequality.[5]

Such — in grossly reductive form — is the genealogy often proposed for Leavis's quarrel with literary theory. As Nairn writes, in perhaps the most hostile assessment to date: 'lunatic empiricism is the perfect psychological and pedagogic match for romantic conservatism. It destroys the intellect, to render the thaumaturgic power of Literature even greater. By extirpating the slightest temptation to abstract thought, it guarantees the onward flow of Organic Community for another few years.'[6] Leavis's work can then be seen as one more example of that will to mystify the politics of criticism by fixing its sights on a long-lost age of 'organic' cultural values. Certainly this nostalgic desire is strong in Leavis's criticism, deriving as it does from Eliot's idea of a 'dissociation of sensibility' that overtook the English mind at around the time of the Civil War, and which henceforth left its debilitating mark on poetry and politics alike.[7] This potent mythology clearly determined the shape of Leavis's canonical 'tradition', as well as the distinctive emphases of his practical criticism. Thus the touchstone of sensuous 'enactment' in poetry — that language should communicate not only ideas but the experience of thinking concretely in visual, tactile, even 'muscular' images — goes along with Leavis's express conviction that the early seventeenth century (the age of Shakespeare and Donne) was the high point of English poetic tradition. As with Eliot, the effect is to focus attention on precisely the kind of poetry that best responds to such preconceived notions of aesthetic value.

So it is that Milton has to be 'dislodged' from his place in the great tradition, apparently because (as Keats had once found) his latinate diction and high epic style were too remote from the native resources of English in its true 'exploratory-creative' character.[8] In fact Leavis's attitude to Milton (like Eliot's before him) was consistent with that same historical *parti pris* that locates the origin of all our modern woes in the Civil War period and the first articulations of opposed class-interest in the politics of popular revolt. When Leavis writes about Shelley there is a similar move to preclude any questions of political alignment by focusing on the poet's stylistic shortcomings, his failure to achieve the kind of sensuous enactment — the vividly realised images and metaphors — that characterise the poetry of Donne and his peers.[9] Thus Shelley's 'immaturity' can be seen on the one hand as a case of individual arrested development, and on the other as somehow symptomatic of poetry's plight in an era of advanced 'dissociation' between thought and sensibility. Here, as with Milton, there is not the least hint that this antipathy might have something to do with these poets' political interests, their belonging to a radical-republican line of descent utterly remote from Eliot's conservative or classicist tradition.

It is one great virtue of recent critical theory to have brought these ideological dimensions more clearly into view. Paul de Man has shrewdly analysed the ways in which a certain phenomenalist aesthetics — an habitual confusion of linguistic with natural or sensory experience — goes along with that deep-laid 'resistance to theory' which typifies conservative thinking about art and cultural politics.[10] De Man nowhere mentions Leavis but his arguments are fully borne out by the constant link between 'sensuous enactment' and that backward-looking vision of a lost 'organic' community which Leavis calls up to support his diagnosis of present-day cultural ills. His version of literary history — the 'line of wit' that runs from Donne to Marvell, then (with various qualifications) from Pope to Keats, Hopkins and Eliot — is so constructed as precisely to exclude those poets, like Milton and Shelley, who resist the values and presuppositions of this powerful aesthetic creed. Thus Keats (for instance) figures in the Leavisian canon as a signal exception to the general rule, a poet whose language transcends the conditions of 'dissociated sensibility' through his cleaving to the vivid particularities of sensuous experience. Hence the famous passage from *Revaluation*, analysing Keats's lines from the 'Ode To Autumn' ('And sometimes, like a gleaner, thou dost keep/Steady thy laden head across a brook') in terms of their physically enacting the effort of muscular balance through the skilful use of enjambement.[11] Unlike Shelley, Keats holds out against the pressures of ideological seduction and the consequent drift toward an abstract imagery remote from living perception.

Leavis's persistent refusal to theorise can therefore be linked to the systematic pattern of inclusions and exclusions which make up his idea of English poetic tradition. It is a pattern that follows from two main imperatives: that history should be seen under the mythical aspect of long-term secular decline, and that poetry should answer to the aims and techniques of a criticism which passes directly from detailed verbal analysis to questions of moral valuation. Such was the purpose of some early essays in *Scrutiny*, setting out the terms for a practical criticism that would go beyond mere close reading to the stage of comparing texts (for instance, poems by Tennyson, Hardy and Lawrence) in point of their 'sincerity', 'maturity' and power to resist an otherwise facile sentimental appeal.[12] Here we can observe with some precision the movement of thought identified by de Man as the source of that 'aesthetic ideology' which conflates linguistic meaning with natural perception and so short-circuits the process of critical thought. 'The link between literature (as art), epistemology, and ethics is the burden of aesthetic theory at least since Kant. It is because we teach literature as an aesthetic function that we can move so easily from literature to its apparent prolongations in the spheres of self-knowledge, of religion, and of politics.'[13] The discourse of aesthetic value carries along with it a tendency to blur distinctions, to accept — as a matter of principled belief — that language can indeed hand across sensations bodily, or 'enact' those meanings that would otherwise belong to the realm of mere abstract representation. It involves, that is to say, a deep-seated resistance to any theory that threatens to block or to complicate the passage from phenomenal experience to linguistic sense.

De Man sees this doctrine as having taken hold through a failure to reckon with the problems encountered in the course of Kant's attempt to make good such claims. His own deconstructive reading of the *Critique of judgement* argues that language simply *won't do* what Kant (or, more properly, the subsequent misreaders of Kant) require of it; namely, achieve a kind of hypostatic union where concepts merge with sensuous intuitions and all ontological distinctions at last fall away. It is a main function of literary theory to 'raise the unavoidable question whether aesthetic values can be compatible with the linguistic structures that make up the entities from which these values are derived'.[14] Furthermore, 'the professing of literature ought to take place under the aegis of this question', since it has been widely and effectively concealed by doctrines that equate the very nature, specifity or value of 'literary' language with its power to communicate sensory perceptions as if by a species of phenomenal enactment. De Man finds this doctrine most typically embodied in the Formalist idea of aesthetic 'defamiliarisation'; the claim that poetry works to revitalise our jaded, routine, everyday habits of perception by forcing us — through metaphor and other such devices — to break with those habits and see things radically anew. This idea he regards as in many ways admirable, but as none the less premised on a simplified and overly dogmatic view of the relation between linguistic structures and aesthetic values. What literary theory brings out, according to de Man, is 'that their compatibility, or lack of it, has to remain an open question and that the manner in which the teaching of literature, since its beginning in the later nineteenth century, has foreclosed the question is unsound, even if motivated by the best intentions'.[15]

Leavis's doctrine of sensuous 'enactment' has much in common with the Formalist emphasis on language in its defamiliarising aspect. In both cases there is the firmly-held conviction that poetry gives access (a special kind of access) to realities otherwise obscured or unperceived through the veil of customary language-habit. In both, there is the further *ethical* claim that such stripping-away of routine perceptions is also, intrinsically, a measure of aesthetic worth and a source of those values attributed to literature by critics convinced of its high moral purpose. So the Formalist position joins up readily enough with Leavis's stress on 'maturity', 'life' and those other evaluative key-terms which enable criticism assuredly to distinguish the good from the bad, or poetry that truly manifests the 'exploratory-creative' use of language from that which merely evokes a false or sentimental response. For Leavis, the common pursuit of such judgements is the only proper business of criticism, and any theory that gets in the way of this pursuit is an idle distraction. Thus one finds him, in an otherwise admiring review of *Seven types of ambiguity*, wondering whether Empson's extraordinary powers of verbal analysis — his sheer ingenuity as a close reader — might not have adversely affected his critical judgement.[16] What Leavis uneasily responds to in Empson's writing is a variant of that same 'dissociation of sensibility' which he, like Eliot, finds everywhere at work in the history of modern (post-enlightenment) thought. It is the way that Empson's readings — especially his pages on Shakespeare, Donne and other canonical poets — press far beyond any possible *correspondence* between linguistic structures, on the one hand, and sensuous intuitions on the other. For Leavis, such semantic agility always carries the threat that language may be seen to generate a signifying surplus irreducible to any kind of straightforward phenomenalist reckoning.

It is therefore no coincidence that his review of *Seven types* appeared shortly after a stocktaking article on Joyce's work-in-progress toward *Finnegans Wake*.[17] Here also, Leavis diagnosed the signs of a growing rift between mere semantic ingenuity and the proper, 'mature' or responsible use of the novelist's linguistic resources. The point could best be made, he argued, by contrasting Joyce's extravagant form of punning virtuosity — 'fit material for the knowing exegete' — with that other, creative-exploratory style of which Shakespeare was the obvious paradigm. By lending itself so readily to 'knowing' exegesis, to criticism of the kind exemplified by Empson's *Seven types*, this new text of Joyce served only to confirm what Leavis perceived as a deepening crisis in the relations of 'thought' and 'sensibility'. At this point, again, we might turn to de Man for a better understanding of Leavis's negative and markedly defensive response. What distinguishes *true* close reading, de Man argues, is its power to unsettle those deep-laid aesthetic and ethical assumptions which have so far governed just about every modern school of critical thought. 'Mere reading, it turns out, prior to any theory, is able to transform critical discourse in a manner that would appear deeply subversive to those who think of the teaching of literature as a substitute for the teaching of theology, ethics, psychology, or intellectual history.' And again: 'close reading accomplishes this in spite of itself because it cannot fail to respond to structures of language which it is the more or less secret aim of literary teaching to keep hidden'.[18] For it is the presence of these aberrant signifying structures — brought to light with such disturbing frequency in the work of a critic like Empson — which threatens to undo the assured correspondence between language and sensuous intuition.

Of course it may be answered that Leavis never thought of criticism or the teaching of literature as a 'substitute' for anything else; that indeed he went further than Arnold, Eliot or any previous critic in his sense of its absolute value and centrality as a humanising discipline of thought. But this would be to miss the

point of de Man's argument. What is at stake in Leavis's pedagogic enterprise is precisely that potent 'aesthetic ideology', that
desire to elide differences and pass directly from sensuous cogni-
tions to judgements of value, which marks the widespread
resistance to theory in modern literary studies. It goes along with a
mythic organicist view of cultural history and a programme of
'practical criticism' which in fact, by its strongly empiricist or
phenomenalist cast, works to exclude those kinds of rigorous close-
reading that would call its most basic values into question. Hence
de Man's claim, in one of his posthumously published essays, that
'those who reproach literary theory for being oblivious to social
and historical (that is to say, ideological) reality are merely stating
their fear at having their own ideological mystifications exposed by
the tool they are trying to discredit. They are, in short, very poor
readers of Marx's *German Ideology*'.[19]

One effect of such demystifying arguments is to show up the
partisan or value-laden character of Leavis's 'tradition', the ways
in which it operates to marginalise those poets (like Milton and
Shelley) who don't fit in with the dominant (post-Eliot) consensus
view. Thus one finds a strong counter-tradition already taking
shape, a line that runs roughly from Spenser, through Milton to
the Romantics (especially Shelley), and thence to Wallace Stevens
and the American heirs of a modernism distinctly unindebted to
Eliot's example.[20] Its co-ordinates are fixed at a maximum remove
from that version of literary history whose outline was sketched
programmatically by Eliot and developed in detail by Leavis. And
this follows very largely from the new understanding of Romanticism to be found in critics like de Man, Geoffrey Hartman and
Harold Bloom; an understanding whose source is the increased
attentiveness to issues of language and representation brought
about by recent post-structuralist theory. Its effects are most
evident in Shelley's case, where the old standard charges — of
poetic immaturity, blurred or unfocused imagery, metaphorical
self-indulgence and so forth — have now given way to detailed
explorations of the way his poetry persistently confronts the
aporias of language, memory and representation.[21] And this in
turn forms part of a wider revaluative project, one that implicitly
questions every aspect of the Eliot–Leavis canonical view.

Michael Bell's study is far from underwriting this general diagnosis of the Leavis 'case'. It is argued from a standpoint of broad
agreement and sympathy with Leavis's aims, though not without
certain clearly-stated reservations, some of them bearing on points

raised here. Most importantly, Bell is willing to press questions —
'theoretical', even 'philosophical' questions — that Leavis would
have thought quite irrelevant to the purposes of authentic literary
criticism. Particularly striking is Bell's extended comparison with
Heidegger's late texts on language, poetry and the limits of analytic reason, a comparison which goes some way toward explaining
Leavis's own, more dogmatic resistance to theory. Again, Bell
strongly contests the idea that Leavis should be seen as a last-ditch
bourgeois ideologue, using his mystified conceptions of language,
creativity and 'organic' values merely to fend off the perceived
threat of an opposing (historical-materialist) analysis. Such arguments, according to Bell, merely confirm what Leavis had to say
about the worsening state of present-day intellectual culture. 'One
may, of course, dissent from Leavis's view of language, or even
find it beneath discussion, but it is the ground of his practice and
Anderson's ignoring of it is symptomatic and characteristic.' The
same would no doubt apply to much of what I have written in this
Foreword. Yet when he touches (for instance) on Leavis's attitude
to Milton — on its background of cultural presuppositions and the
various counter-arguments advanced by dissenting commentators
— Bell goes far toward providing an alternative, more subtly
nuanced critique.

So far there has been an almost complete lack of dialogue
between those who have lined up squarely behind Leavis, endors-
ing his attitudes as a matter of faith, and those (like Anderson and
Nairn) who have taken a sharply diagnostic view. And this antago-
nism has found an institutional echo in those numerous university
Departments of English where 'theory' is grudgingly admitted to
the syllabus as a thing quite apart from 'practical criticism' or the
interests of better, more intelligent reading. Bell's study leaves no
doubt of Leavis's role in maintaining and promoting this widespread attitude. But it should also do much to persuade the
unprejudiced reader that the only way beyond this divisive situation is a genuine effort to comprehend the sources of Leavis's
potent and continuing influence.

Christopher Norris

1

Introduction

Most existing accounts of Leavis have chosen one of the following emphases. Those which engage substantively with his judgements tend to accept the general premises of his critical practice. Others which concentrate on his discourse and procedure from a principled point of view are more often expressing some fundamental disagreement or scepticism.[1] There is, therefore a mainly negative cast to such principled accounts. It is quite understandable that anyone who accepts the terms of Leavis's judgements will feel less reason to elucidate them theoretically; and particularly so in view of his own well-known belief that the practice of criticism is not significantly aided, or undermined, by theoretical articulation. But the outcome is that while there are several extended and percipient studies of Leavis which follow, and indeed combine, these interests, his critical procedure has not been closely considered in a way that encompasses his commitments and premises. There is a danger that inappropriate methodological criteria will become the orthodox means of describing his practice.

Hence this essay has a different focus. In the brief annotated bibliography I list several studies which have already collectively covered Leavis's critical career, his historical context and his implicit theoretical stance. I address these considerations more synoptically and give instead an intensive reading to some representative essays with a view to analysing their principled methods in relation to their judgemental force. The emphasis of this reading, in other words, will be not expository, or theoretical, so much as critical in something like the sense we apply to writing about literature. Leavis's discourse constantly raises the question of an appropriate mode for the discussion of literature. In poetry we accept as a matter of course shifts, doublings, affirmations and suggestions which philosophical discourse, for example, would not normally tolerate. Leavis's critical language is not poetry; far from it, some would say. But he had a seriously considered view of how it might properly reflect the nature of literary or 'creative' expression. He was aware that a critic may say many true things about the work of literature and yet fail to address what really matters. We can explicate technique and meaning while missing the significance. If this is an implicit standard for the critic, then it remains the standard for any attempt to appreciate the critic's own practice. I wish, therefore, to consider Leavis's critical rhetoric and premises, in the light of his purposes and achievement.

I believe there is a further, more implicit, value in such an enquiry. Leavis had a powerful, personal vision of English literature as part of English language and history. As will become apparent, I do not share his whole conception or agree with all his judgements. But he expresses a classic view. That is to say, a view one needs to appreciate in its full force and cogency; particularly if one wishes to dissent from it. And to call it classic is to shift the emphasis from its personal dimension. As he frequently noted, the most impressively personal achievements in literature are often the most representative. And that suggests how emphasis on the personal stamp of his own criticism can be misleading. For some version of his stance effectively underlies, in suffused and implicit ways, much of the everyday reading, and study, of literature; even where this is overtly denied. Furthermore, his characteristic concern was not for an 'original' interpretation, or 'approach', but for probing the subliminal processes underlying the most common readings. Hence the double irony with which he uses the term 'common place'. I believe, therefore, that some of the difficulties which have been seen in Leavis's procedures are not personal, but generic. Rather than creating unnecessary difficulties for himself, he has made intrinsic ones properly salient. The consequence is that in analysing his rhetoric and method I will be engaging much of the time with the generic nature of literary criticism. In short, my attempt to explicate his personal conception will, inevitably, present him as an especially penetrative and self-conscious example of the act of reading.

2
Life and Work

Frank Raymond Leavis was born on 14 July 1895; roughly a decade after T. S. Eliot, James Joyce, D. H. Lawrence and Ezra Pound. His father ran a bicycle shop in Cambridge, the town in which Leavis was to live and work throughout his life. He was educated at the Perse school under the headmastership of W. H. D. Rouse who was noted for his teaching of classical Greek by the direct method. Leavis took a serious enough interest in languages to add Italian in later years to his school knowledge of French and German, although in view of his special commitment to his native literary tradition, and his belief that it was the only one on which he could speak authoritatively, his reading in these languages is not very evident in his published criticism. It does, however, have a bearing on his sense of the English language as the medium in which the native literary tradition was produced. He saw this literature as pre-eminent in the quality of its emotional and ethical intelligence, and his concern for language as the medium, and index, of experience is central to that claim.

When the Great War started in 1914 Leavis refused to kill and served instead as a medical orderly at the front. His objection was on 'conscientious' rather than religious grounds and he had doubt-less inherited the cultivated, secular outlook of his father for whom he had considerable respect. Leavis brought to the reading of literature such a serious and complete ethical vision that it has often been seen as a religious one. The analogy is helpful provided Leavis's outlook is not understood as merely an ethical afterglow of religious belief. His agnosticism is as primary as his ethical and spiritual seriousness. That is important to the distinctive edge of his critical vision which is not to be confused with a simple moralism.

The experience of the front, including gas, permanently damaged his health. The moral and intellectual effects of the war are harder to determine since he himself tended to view those years as 'the great hiatus'. But clearly its impact was not to produce the moral conversion of, say, Siegfried Sassoon so much as to intensify and mature the ethical and social concern he subsequently brought to the reading of literature and particularly modern literature.

In 1919 he returned to Cambridge and started reading for a degree at Emmanuel College initially in History and then, after the first year, in English. The English School at Cambridge had only been established in 1917 and the lecturers at that stage were drawn mainly from other subject areas such as history or classics. This reflects the distinctive aim of the School which was to read the vernacular literature with a contemporary critical purpose rather than with the scholarly emphasis that dominated other university degrees in English. Although Leavis had only a relatively humble position at Cambridge through most of his teaching life, it is he who most clearly exemplifies what such a contemporary critical concern might be like. He presented in 1924 a PhD thesis on 'The relationship of journalism to literature: studied in the rise and earlier development of the press in England'. The title 'Dr' became common in addressing, or referring to, him and in so far as he endorsed this practice it emphasised that he had indeed conducted a research thesis and that his objection to much scholarly activity was not an objection to scholarship *per se* but to scholarship not informed by a critical purpose.

In 1927 Leavis was appointed to a probationary lectureship in English to teach for the university without attachment to a college. Over the next few years he started to publish book reviews for *The Cambridge Review* but his primary commitment was clearly to teaching. When his first substantial publications began to appear a few years later, not only their subject-matter but their whole style and method were formed by the demands of teaching which includes the use of the teacher's own personality. His written style is, among other things, an attempt to convey on the page the personal and momentary nature of literary recognition.

One of his students was Queenie Dorothy Roth, whom he married in 1929 and who became his most productive and long-standing collaborator. Q. D. Leavis, indeed, wrote a substantial body of criticism of her own, despite, as she was wont to point out, the responsibilities of caring for a young family on a small income. From her research days onwards she read voluminously in fiction, particularly by female writers both major and minor from the late eighteenth century onwards. F.R.L.'s growing interest in the novel over the thirties and forties was influenced by her long-standing commitment to it. He always insisted on the importance of her contribution to their joint work and on her unrecognised pre-eminence, in his view, as a contemporary critic of the novel. There is, therefore, danger of perpetuating an injustice by entitling this work merely *F. R. Leavis*. There could no doubt be another study entitled *The Leavises*. But the emphasis of the present study is on the conception underlying the critical achievement and for this purpose F.R.L. provides the best focus. Their successful collaboration was a result not just of their similarity but also of their complementary natures. Q.D.L. wrote with a direct trenchancy whereas F.R.L. had an inwardly turned deliberativeness that grew more marked in his later years. This was partly because of a felt need to ground the significance of his critical activity while performing it. And likewise it was F.R.L. who took occasion to articulate most explicitly their common conception. His critical exclusiveness in meditating on what he saw as the absolutely important writers is another aspect of this intensive concentration on the essential. It is, therefore, in Leavis himself that we can most closely identify and appreciate the given conception.

In 1930 Leavis published two pamphlet-sized works, *Mass civilization and minority culture* and *D. H. Lawrence*. The former set out the cultural-historical critique underlying the Leavises' criticism of literature and it drew strongly on the research thesis of Queenie Leavis published separately as *Fiction and the reading public* (1932). In their view the extension of literacy and the commercial production of popular reading-matter had increasingly overwhelmed the capacity, individually or communally, to recognise serious creative work. The corollary of the Leavises' strong belief in the significance of creative literature as a means of understanding individual and social experience was the belief that a merely sentimental pulp literature was actively pernicious. Q. D. Leavis traced this process through the rise of the eighteenth-century novel of sentiment and included Dickens as an example of the progressive debasement of taste. By the twentieth century there was no forum left in which serious, important work could be discussed and recognised. The first function of an English school, of course, should be to provide such a forum although Leavis soon recognised that his academic colleagues were not willing, or able, to do this with the stringency that he saw as required.

The pamphlet on D. H. Lawrence, who died in that year, concerned a writer who had not been given adequate recognition in his lifetime. At this point Leavis was aware of the problems and failures in Lawrence but was not yet able to weigh them against the positive achievement. Only later did he come to see a representative importance in Lawrence's cultural critique. The principal interest of the pamphlet now is in showing that his later commitment to Lawrence followed a clear awareness of the standard objections.

In 1932, an important year for Leavis, he was appointed director of studies in English at Downing College where he continued to teach for the next thirty years, and in the same year the journal *Scrutiny* was founded. He joined the editorial board in time for its third number and before long it was Leavis who gave the journal its distinctive and influential stamp. *Scrutiny* provided the forum already mentioned for identifying important contemporary work and for reviewing the traditional canon by comparably serious criteria. Some of the authors found wanting by Leavis, such as Joyce, Auden or Shelley have remained a matter of dispute, but the authors on whom he focused positively, who include Pope, Blake, Wordsworth, George Eliot and T. S. Eliot, are seen in the light of Leavis's powerful vision of literature as a primordial and holistic form of understanding. Furthermore, his criticism was informed by a teacher's concern to present the essential to students with limited time and experience even if it was not formally addressed to students but to their tutors. Hence Leavis's impact on his own students was extended through *Scrutiny* to a wider circle of undergraduates and school teachers. In this way he had a decisive influence on the school teaching and the undergraduate reading of literature even while his effect on university teaching remained limited.

This same year also saw the publication of *New bearings in English poetry* and *How to teach reading: a primer for Ezra Pound*. *New bearings* was his first major volume of criticism. His own critical understanding was formed partly in attempting to come to terms with the modern movement; particularly, at first, the poetry. The terms of a previous criticism were not adequate to the new occasions as will be seen in detail later. This study, devoted principally to Hopkins, Yeats, Pound and Eliot, is an attempt to identify the essential new achievements in modern poetry. It is notable, therefore, that Pound is given mainly negative attention in this volume. Leavis admired *Hugh Selwyn Mauberley* and Pound's tough-minded iconoclasm with respect to the British literary ambience before the war. But even that quality in Pound was the obverse of a fundamental insensitivity in Leavis's eyes and *How to teach reading*, offered as a reply to Pound's *ABC of reading*, indicates what he objected to. It was the preoccupation with technique along with, and related to, Pound's rootlessly synoptic, cosmopolitan conception of the literary past. Hopkins, Yeats and Eliot were all technical innovators but this, in Leavis's view, was only significant in the light of the expressive needs by which they were impelled.

In 1933 he published a collection of his early *Scrutiny* essays under the title *For continuity* and also the small volume *Culture and environment*, a collection of school discussion exercises drawn up with his former student Denys Thompson who was now a school-teacher. These were passages with questions designed to promote thought about developments in the social culture at large as manifest in representative uses of language. In the same year he edited, with an introduction, *Towards standards of criticism*. This was a selection of essays from the journal *The Calendar of Modern Letters* which had run from 1925 to 1927 under the editorship of Edgell Rickword, providing a forum for a younger generation of writers seeking to reassess their immediate heritage. It ran a series of pieces under the heading 'Scrutinies' in which older writers such as Bennett and Galsworthy were given close critical attention by their younger contemporaries. The title *Scrutiny* indicated its intention of continuing the function of *The Calendar*.

In the next year he edited *Determinations*, a selection of *Scrutiny* essays by several contributors, and then in 1936 came his next important volume, *Revaluation*. This again was made up of previous essays but it comprised a continuous argument on the evolution of English poetry from the time of Shakespeare till the early nineteenth century. Along with *New bearings* it completed Leavis's essential account of the poetic tradition, a topic to be discussed in Chapter 5. The two major studies of English poetry were to be complemented by three important books on English fiction. His general statement on the English novel appeared in *The great tradition* (1948) and was followed by *D. H. Lawrence: novelist* (1955) and *Dickens the novelist*, in collaboration with Q. D. Leavis (1970). Leavis's reading of English fiction will also be discussed at length, in Chapter 6.

Leavis summed up the long-standing *Scrutiny* campaign for changes in education with *Education and the university* (1943). The British political climate was sympathetic to radical change and to prospective renewal in the post-war years. Butler's Education Act was passed in 1944 setting up the tripartite school system which dominated British secondary education until into the 1960s. A minority of pupils were identified at an early age as able to benefit and were sent to academic 'grammar' schools or to 'technical' schools while the rest of the school population attended the inevitably less prestigious 'secondary modern' schools. The intention was to give an appropriate education to all children irrespective of social or financial advantage. In the event the social divisions actually encouraged by this system coupled with its dependence on such an early and total division of the school population made it politically intolerable as well as educationally controversial. Leavis himself disclaimed any significant expertise with respect to the teaching of schoolchildren but his conception of an intellectual clerisy, not governing so much as serving the nation, was very much of the grammar school era.

His direct concern was with the universities. In an article of 1940 he had set out a number of principles for the teaching of English literature at university level.[1] These included: concentration on literary sensitivity as well as factual knowledge; the introduction of assessed course essays to replace some of the final examinations; a strong element of 'practical criticism' in examination papers; connections to be explored with other fields such as history or philosophy; the practice of a foreign language; the abandoning of compulsory Anglo-Saxon to make room for these lateral studies; and teaching through small seminar groups rather than individual tutorials. He even suggested, with an openness of spirit that belies his later reputation for conservative strictness, that students be encouraged to undertake risky and speculative topics or, as he put it, to have 'the ability to skip and scamper with wisdom and conscience'. The interest of these proposals now is that they have all been adopted by the modern British universities founded in the 1960s and, of course, by many of the older establishments too. Yet Leavis opposed this expansion of university education since the traditional assumption of students' own responsibility in 'reading' a subject would not survive large scale, mixed-ability teaching. And the single one of his proposals that has not been generally adopted indicates the profound difference in spirit here. This was a suggestion for a special paper on the seventeenth century as the historical period in which the crucial formation of modern culture occurred. Leavis clearly intended that his critical vision of the origins of modern culture would be the ultimate focus of literary education. But the principle that governs modern literary study at degree level is rather of education as a neutral resource. Individual tutors or courses may embody strongly particular views but the strategy, or accepted effect, of the whole is to avoid as far as possible any over-arching interpretation. The relativism of this is not what Leavis intended. Ironically, perhaps, he spent the early part of his career wishing to 'modernise' the study of literature and the latter part of it opposing the form that modernisation took when it occurred. His own positive ideal was different from each.

His conception was that a university should not just be a place of training and enquiry in separate disciplines but the active centre for an overall assessment of contemporary life. Underlying all academic specialisms, Leavis argued, there is the prior cultural achievement of language. Language, in his view, is not a detachable instrument of thought and communication. It is the historical embodiment of its community's assumptions and aspirations at levels which are so subliminal much of the time that language is their only index. The various specialist disciplines have, of course, their appropriate terminologies but these are not, except by a deeply misleading metaphor, separate *languages*. Hence the critical study of language is the arena in which the community's fundamental values can be holistically understood. The English school, which is concerned with the most complex and consummate uses of language, was for Leavis the appropriate forum for this.

In 1950 he edited *Mill on Bentham and Coleridge* with an introduction in which he set out the historical importance of utilitarian thought. Bentham epitomised the scientistic drift of modern culture and social thinking which was, in Leavis's view, the radical enemy of the holistic, humane understanding he desiderated. It should be said that in so far as Bentham was addressing himself to the specifically legislative domain this may be unfair to him. In that context individual human happiness may properly be regarded as a kind of algebraical *x* which the law must take account of but cannot directly determine or evaluate. At the same time, he showed little real awareness of the limitation of his terms and Leavis's true concern is with the historical impact of his mode of thinking. Hence the 'technological-Benthamite' became his shorthand reference for the characteristic malaise of modern culture.

Two years later another collection of his *Scrutiny* essays appeared under the title *The common pursuit*. This is his best-known and most influential collection of essays outside the volumes on English poetry and the novel. In the following year *Scrutiny* ceased publication. The difficulties of running the journal, still without institutional or financial support, during the war and the post-war years had been considerable for the Leavises. Other nuclear contributors were no longer in Cambridge and there is a discernible falling off in quality over the second decade of its production. More speculatively, it may be surmised that a journal with such a clearly defined programme and closely shared premisses was in increasing danger of becoming repetitive; an imitation of its best self.

Leavis became a figure of national notoriety in 1962 when his Richmond lecture, 'Two cultures? The significance of C. P. Snow', was delivered at Downing College and subsequently published in *The Spectator*. Charles Snow's Rede lecture 'The two cultures and the scientific revolution' (1959) had proposed that as a matter of educational policy practitioners of the scientific and humanistic disciplines should have some intelligent awareness of each others' specialisms. That has never been a matter of significant dispute. But he argued this case by suggesting that these two broad areas of enquiry constitute two separate, equal cultures so that an ignorance of twentieth-century physics was comparable to an ignorance of Shakespeare. That in itself was directly contrary to Leavis's view of language as the embodiment of a common culture. But in fact Snow's treatment of his two cultures, while formally regarding them as equal, clearly favoured 'scientific culture' over the supposedly obscurantist tendency of literary people. It was clear to Leavis that 'literary culture' meant nothing more to Snow than the conventional cultivation of polite letters. Yet the fact that Snow had published a number of works of fiction lent to his views the implied authority of a literary practitioner. Indeed, by 1962 the Rede lecture was in its sixth reprinting and was, Leavis claimed, being mentioned approvingly by candidates seeking entrance to the university. As it happened, this was also the moment when a massive expansion of British tertiary education was about to be launched and the conceptions embodied in the Rede lecture seemed to Leavis not only wrong but to have a canonical self-assurance. Accordingly he attacked the idea of the two cultures; the literary standing of Snow which was an implicit premiss of his authority; and the whole mode of utterance Snow employed. What was at stake for Leavis was not particular propositions advanced by Snow, but the whole relation to language from which these propositions emerged. The Richmond lecture, therefore, includes a summative statement of Leavis's conception of the function of criticism in the community at large. He did not believe that critics, any more than great artists, have necessarily any special wisdom to offer but they could collaboratively uphold a criterion of holistic awareness in discourse.

The year of the Richmond lecture saw also the termination of his university readership and Downing fellowship although he had an honorary fellowship for the next two years. From then on he had visiting positions at several British universities including Bristol, the University of Wales and York. The Clark lectures delivered at Cambridge in 1967 were published as *English literature in our time and the university* (1969). *Lectures in America* (1969) was a joint volume based on lectures given by both the Leavises at American universities in 1966.

Three final volumes of essays appeared in the seventies: *Nor shall my sword* (1972), *The living principle* (1975) and *Thought, words and creativity* (1976). Although Leavis did not relinquish criticism in his later years, as is evident from *'Anna Karenina' and other essays* (1967) and *Dickens the novelist* (1970), he clearly felt a greater necessity to defend his activity in more general terms. He sought corroboration for his holistic sense of language and understanding in the works of Marjorie Grene and Michael Polanyi. The titles of their best-known works, respectively *The knower and the known* and *Personal knowledge*, suggest their common recognition of the personal factors in understanding even in scientific domains. This general endeavour is not, I think, the strongest part of Leavis's *œuvre*. Despite his power as a polemicist his best cultural criticism is to be found in his literary critical practice. His later essays in cultural criticism derive their authoritative implication from Leavis's already classic critique of English literature.

F. R. Leavis died in 1978 having been made a Companion of Honour in the New Year. Q. D. Leavis died in 1981.

3

The Arnoldian Heritage and the Modern World

Leavis is the principal twentieth-century descendant of the English literary critical tradition in which Dr Johnson, Wordsworth, Coleridge and Matthew Arnold are among his most notable forebears. Arnold was Leavis's most immediately pertinent predecessor in his concern for 'the function of criticism' in the modern world and Arnold's formula that 'poetry is a criticism of life' encapsulates much of the distinctive character of this tradition; especially its subordination of speculative issues to a trenchant sense of moral purpose. The best way of understanding the intellectual and historical matrix in which Leavis's criticism was formed is to see him as the focal point of tension between this Arnoldian heritage and the demands placed on it by the literary and social circumstances of the early twentieth century. These demands were partly destructive of the tradition and partly transformative of it. In Leavis this tradition was forced to re-examine its first principles and the purpose of the present study is to suggest in what ways, and with what measure of continuing pertinence, he met that challenge.

The critical impact of Leavis lies not in a complexity of ideas *about* literature so much as in the quality of attention *to* it. The distinction matters particularly in his case because of his conviction that theoretical preoccupations should be kept not merely distinct, but strictly apart, from the judgemental activity of criticism. In his view, explicit theorising is not only unnecessary to critical practice but is, or tends to be, actively pernicious. It distracts or confuses while performing no essential function. That is to put in very bald terms, although no more so than Leavis himself when addressing the issue conceptually, what is manifestly a problematic distinction. Much depends on the precise nature and quality of the activities covered by these terms and it will take some time to unpack what is at stake in them for Leavis. In his exchange with René Wellek in which Leavis refused to give a theoretical, or even a principled, account of his critical practice he was speaking theoretically *malgré lui* and his response was negative and pragmatic.[1] But Wellek's questions about criticism did not address themselves to the nature of literature itself. Leavis's criticism involves an ambitious claim for literature upon which in turn the understanding of the critical act is contingent. It is only in terms of his overall premiss about the nature of literature that we can adequately assess his stance.

Now in a general way this suspicion of theoretical analysis is a quintessentially English quality in Leavis. It goes back through Dr Johnson's legendary appeal to experience over theory by kicking a stone to refute David Hume's philosophical scepticism. The empirical and intuitional bases of Leavis's critical practice have become a principal locus of disagreement respecting the present viability of his example. For a succinct critique of Leavis's anti-theoretical stance the reader may consult the relevant section of Perry Anderson's essay 'Components of the national culture'.[2] In a more positive reading of Leavis and of the larger tradition to which he belongs, Fred Inglis's *Radical earnestness* brings out the historical contexts in which this mode of criticism is to be understood.[3] In the Johnsonian instance there is a simple inability to recognise a philosophical issue. The difficulty with Leavis is to decide whether he is in the same way sub-theoretical or whether, as he believed, he was performing a function that is legitimately elusive of theoretical definition. Is he below or above such theoretical accounting? He undoubtedly shared something of Johnson's common-sense indifference to philosophy but the challenge of the modern context obliged him to meditate on the nature of literature in a fundamental way that Johnson did not. Leavis's direct statements on the theoretical domain were, as I have suggested, largely negative. They are attempts to ward off rather than to engage such discussion. He saw the domain of theory not only as too generalised, which is the principal answer he gave to Wellek, but also, we might say, as epi-phenomenal, or secondary, to experience. The truths or principles that matter to us, even when couched in a theoretical way, are those which experience endorses. The apparent authority of theory rests on a prior commonality of experience. Another way of expressing the same recognition is Leavis's insistence that the specialised 'languages' of intellectual disciplines ultimately derive from the underlying source of the common tongue. His own account of the English critical tradition reflects that emphasis.

He wrote separate essays on his principal forebears: Johnson, Coleridge, Arnold and T. S. Eliot.[4] While he has reservations about each of them, his positive comments could in many cases be applied to himself and would collectively comprise a fair account of the model, and standard, by which he would wish to be judged. One of his opening comments on Johnson indicates the spirit of his treatment. He applauds in Johnson the classic articulation, and shrewd use, of a deeply considered point of view rather than actually agreeing with Johnson's Augustan outlook. Johnson has no lack of general principles but it is the weight of experience that gives his criticism its cogency even now. And indeed following the same line of thought we might take the very readiness with which Johnson can appeal to principle as an index of his felt commonality of experience with his reader. Leavis clearly saw himself as within a tradition which had undergone constant transformation with the changing experience of the historical culture. But in his own time it seemed to him that the historical pressures within the culture were such as to cause not a further creative transformation of the tradition but its extinction.

In his own day the experiential commonality underpinning this humanistic tradition had begun seriously to break down. When Johnson rejoiced 'to concur with the common reader' he indicated the ultimate criterion for all these critics. They each took the educated common reader as the final, if sometimes rather notional, arbiter of literary judgement. I say 'notional' because the professionally specialised activity of the critic was to form as well as articulate public judgement and that might well involve more immediate disagreements. Hence Johnson's satisfaction at being able wholeheartedly to endorse a judgement already clearly formed. By contrast, Leavis saw in his own day the rapid disappearance of an educated common readership. In the Leavises' view, between the commercialised mass culture that followed on general literacy and highbrow cultural coteries such as the grouping associated with Bloomsbury, there was no public forum at once serious and wide enough to constitute a significant public. And over the course of their academic careers the Leavises saw the extensive institutionalising of vernacular literary studies; a development which, in so far as it was based largely on a scientific model of original research, only exacerbated the absence of such a public by creating an artificial one.

Now whether the disappearance of the 'educated common reader' is indeed a cultural catastrophe is a matter for extensive debate on political control of, and access to, 'culture'. It is, indeed, a matter for historical interpretation whether this common culture actually existed or was itself a persuasive myth. But what is clear is that the kind of cultural consensus necessary to the humanist tradition no longer pertained even as a belief. This is the sense in which the circumstances of the modern world were destructive of the Arnoldian heritage. There is an historical irony here, however. Leavis spent his career as an embattled iconoclast attacking the contemporary world of letters and its principal representatives both within and outside the academic world. Yet in retrospect, precisely because he had to think closely about the nature of literature and criticism, he tends now to be adduced as its representative instance. He provides the most considered case for the humanist tradition at large. I believe that is indeed part of his importance to us now, and to appreciate the force of the case we need to consider not just the destructive impact of modern social culture but the transformative impact of modern literature on the Arnoldian conception in Leavis.

Leavis's hostility to theory may be related, as I have suggested, to a traditional British empiricism. But it may also be related to an important strain running through diverse kinds of literary modernism. Leavis's critical range extended over the whole of post-renaissance English literature but he followed the lead of the modern literary generation, and most notably T. S. Eliot, in considering the past from the viewpoint of a critical concern with the present. His criticism was formed most crucially by his coming to terms with contemporary literature and I believe he remains, despite limitations and partialities, the most important critic *of* that generation as Johnson or Arnold were of theirs. In other words, it is not just that he engaged critically with his great contemporaries but that he was able to do so fruitfully because of his independent commitment to the same set of concerns. And by the same token the literature and the literary thinking of that generation was especially formative of his conception of literature and therefore of criticism.

The particular aspect of the modern movement that I have in mind here is its resistance to the fallacy of paraphrase. As a late transformation of the romantic impulse it preserved, albeit in its own ways, a sense of the privileged and irreducible nature of poetic utterance or symbol. Having shed some of the more mystical claims of an earlier romanticism and given a sharp technical attention to language as the locus of meaning, writers of this generation were particularly conscious of the potency generated within the poetic formulation. And this is reflected not just in the hostility to paraphrase or the refusal to reduce literary meaning to a moral idea. It manifests itself as a resistance to the realm of discursive ideas at large as opposed to the direct apprehension of complex experience enabled by literary language.

Hence, for example, T. S. Eliot's complimentary remark on Henry James that he 'had a mind so fine that no idea could violate it'.[5] He was not praising James's intelligence for resisting false or banal ideas. His point was that James's mind showed its quality by not functioning in terms of 'ideas' at all. And indeed James's sinuous prose does seem to avoid settling into the form of ideas even to the extent normally expected of a sentence. His characteristic sentence reads rather as a responsive plasticity following, and recording, the shifts of perception and emphasis as they arise. When the sentence is completed it is like the plaster cast of an ant-hill taken from the inside: firm in its final shape but with that shape determined by the external givens rather than by its own imposed logic. The case of James is particularly relevant since his prose seems to be the nearest model for Leavis's own which reflects a similar suspicion of the reductive and the generalised. But the fundamental attitude at stake here is echoed in other writers of this generation as in Yeats's dictum that we can 'embody' truth but not 'know' it or in Lawrence's defnition of thought as 'man in his wholeness, wholly attending'.

The common thread in the several comments quoted here is the belief that true understanding is manifest in a participatory responsiveness to the object. And in so far as 'thinking' implies a parallel structure of ideas it may actually impede rather than focus the act of attention. It may provide an unwitting substitute for the true object. Now there are, of course, enormous difficulties of a philosophical kind in such an account of thinking or language. Words, for one thing, *are* ideas. Maybe we should understand it, in part at least, not as a definition but as a stylistic purpose and disposition. It is not so much a definition of language and thought *tout court* as a stylistic principle of leaning against their duplicitous tendencies. Indeed, the question of language is such a large one that it requires extended treatment in the next chapter. For immediate purposes, however, we need to note only that as part of his meditation on the modernist generation in particular Leavis was convinced of a vital but irreducible significance in works of literature. This irreducibility is the crucial premiss for his conception of criticism.

I have said a 'vital' significance since what has just been said about the irreplaceability of the poetic formulation must be taken in conjunction with another aspect of the Arnoldian heritage which is even more strongly manifest in Leavis than it was in Arnold himself. In his essay 'Literature and dogma' Arnold had argued for a new way of responding to the Bible now that scholarship and science had discredited it as a literal historical account of creation. The Bible in Arnold's view had not thereby lost its moral significance as a statement of human and communal meaning. Indeed, with the removal of its supernatural framework it became the supreme and irreplaceable expression of the significance of life as seen by its particular ethnic community. The Bible in effect should be seen as literature; but not as 'mere' literature; rather with literature now assuming something of the burden traditionally borne by religious belief. Instead of 'reflecting' spiritual values and significances it provides their very mode of being. The great authors of the modern movement also saw literature as having this primordial value with respect to the creation and definition of human meaning. Hence the special edge of significance in the irreduciblity of poetic utterance. The significances of art, and particularly the verbal art of literature, are not only unique in kind but may be of a supreme importance.

Leavis is the figure in whom the modernist sense of irreducibility and the Arnoldian sense of significance are most intensely combined; the one, of course, intensifying the other. And this brings us to the more precise appropriateness of the word 'vital' as used above. Arnold argued for the civilising and formative value of great literature and put more 'faith' in this, we might say, than in religion. But his habitual rhetoric implied a confident belief in recognisable, universally compelling values. While notionally according to literature a primary and revelatory significance he treated it still in practice as largely instrumental to the values on which civilised men, the educated common readers, were agreed. As Nietzsche remarked of Arnold's contemporary, George Eliot, she had discarded religion yet carried on as if it were still there.[6] Well, in many ways, as a cultural fact it still was. For Leavis, and for others of his generation such as Lawrence or the later Yeats, religion had ceased to be this inertial cultural fact, and the religious impulse, as the desire to affirm an overall significance in human life, asserted itself with primary urgency in the new terms. Leavis accepted the Arnoldian settlement, therefore, but did so with a seriousness to which Arnold had not been impelled. For Leavis the sense of responsibility and reverence towards an ultimate value was directed not at the divine but at the value of life itself. As with Nietzsche, it would be reductive to call him a 'vitalist' in so far as they both resisted any naïve reification of the vital principle. But for both of them an implicit sense of wholeness and fullness of being guided their cultural criticism. Works of culture either enhance or corrupt the quality of life. In this respect, part of the effect of modernity on the Arnoldian heritage in Leavis was to make him take it with an absolute seriousness. If we use the word 'vital' for Leavis's sense of importance in cultural discriminations it is with a conscious etymological tap-root back to the value of life itself.

To express this transformation of the Arnoldian heritage in more literary critical terms, we may compare it with a classically different model of literary significance. Pope's formulation 'True Wit is Nature to Advantage dressed/What oft was thought but ne'er so well expressed' indicates the degree to which his neo-classical outlook could externalise, at least when conceptualising, the nature of literary meaning. His account contains a lurking problem if one really wants to know what is meant by 'true wit'. The fundamental proposition is actually circular: 'True wit is well expressed'. But we, and Pope, are distracted from this by the confident appeal to 'Nature' as the agreed, self-evident external point of reference. As long as there is a consensus, whether real or convincingly affirmed, about 'Nature' the problem of literary value can remain dormant. Rather than appeal to nature in this direct way, Matthew Arnold developed his 'touchstone' method of adducing classic passages of literature as the exemplary embodiments of literary value. This implies a different, more intrinsic, conception than Pope's. Of course, he is ultimately appealing to nature or 'life' as he might rather say. But by seeking to identify the value in another literary text he is recognising that literary evaluation cannot simply be referred to the more basic category of 'nature'. At the same time there remains in the touchstone method a crucial deflection of essential issues. The moments of consummate past achievement are externally adduced for the immediate critical purpose. The usefulness of the touchstone,

which is predicated on a measure of difference, may be undermined by its inappropriateness. It may not tell us what the
intrinsic value of the new work is. In practice, as a man of wide
reading and shrewd judgement, Arnold exercised a deservedly
influential first-hand criticism of what he read. And as Leavis
himself pointed out in his essay on Arnold he was clearly capable of
performing practical criticism, or close reading, had he wished.
But his formal conception of what he was doing did not oblige him
to account for his judgements in a fully intrinsic way. His view of
Anna Karenina as 'life' rather than 'art' indicates his tendency to
polarise these realms rather than analyse their interaction.

Leavis might be said to have adopted the touchstone method but
with a different emphasis from Arnold's. Part of the difference, of
course, is that Leavis wished to reassess the English literary canon
and therefore proposed some rather different touchstones. But the
more significant difference for present purposes is that he
attempted to penetrate more directly and intrinsically their self-
evident quality. Leavis appealed, for example, to Keats's 'Ode to
Autumn' as a classic, Shakespearean use of the English language
invoking a sensory and emotional complex in an enactive way.
Indeed his way of appealing to sensory quality in the language has
since been questioned and I will return to that general issue in the
next chapter. But this difficulty arises precisely from Leavis's
insistence on locating the qualities in question actually *in* the
language of the poem. Of course, the poem draws on the experience of life as lived under the shadow of mortality but it is not to be
explained by reflections on this. The poem is a unique experience
in itself which quickens our sense of life. What has in effect happened here is a gradual reversal of the logical relation of 'poetry'
and 'nature' as compared to Pope. Rather than there being an
agreed order of values upon which our appreciation of poetry, and
the act of composition, may be said to rest, the poem itself is now
our way of engaging, of getting adequate access to, our evaluative
commitments. The reading of poetry in this conception does not
assume consensus. It is a way of exploring the reality, or the possibility, of a consensus.

To this extent the personal and cultural relativity of literary
judgement was not problematic to Leavis. It was not a difficulty or
an embarrassment for the critic because it was of the essence in
critical activity. Leavis's whole method highlights the implications
of 'literary' judgement. In the ultimately irreducible realm of
fundamental values, literature, as the art whose medium is

language, has a special capacity to create value in the form of knowledge; to enact value in words. The critic is not 'applying' pre-existing 'standards' but participating in the creation of values. In a general way this is not a very unusual belief for a modern literary critic or serious reader to hold. But I have briefly sketched the Arnoldian background and his formative involvement with the modern movement to bring out what is special in Leavis. He brings to the irreducibility of literary utterance a sense of significance for which the word 'religious' is the nearest appropriate term. Hence the difference between Leavis and many other, less controversial, critical practitioners may lie not in any fundamental difference in the principled stance so much as in the frankness and insistence with which he enforces some of the silent premisses of most critical activity. And therein lies much of the importance of his case. In literary criticism, judgements of quality are often conveyed as part of some other argument of an historical or an interpretative kind. This is perfectly legitimate provided that writer and reader are clear with themselves as to what is happening. Indeed, the example of Leavis will perhaps bring home to us the benefits of such an indirect relation to the fundamental. Yet there is clearly a danger in this of failing to engage seriously or at all with the issues of value that underwrite critical activity. Whatever else we may wish to say of him, Leavis was never guilty of that and his example retains its cogency in that respect even if his particular method no longer seems an adequate model. He foregrounded the issue of fundamental value by keeping his eye exclusively on it. To sum the matter up in Leavis's own terms we must read 'literature as literature and not another thing' but there are no 'purely literary values'. To bring out the continuing pertinence of this we may consider two of the most substantial challenges to the Leavisian mode of criticism: Marxism and the search for a 'scientific' method in criticism.

The *Scrutiny* critics devoted considerable energy to exposing the merely conventional and coterie responses which they saw usurping the contemporary function of criticism whether in the academic world or in the national organs of culture such as broadcasting and quality journalism. Yet while this was manifestly important to them as a matter of cultural health it was not of a challenging order intellectually. The truly substantial opponent was recognised in the alternative cultural critique being offered by Marxism. As part of an attempted dialogue, *Scrutiny* published several articles defending the Marxian analysis; notably by A. L.

Morton and H. B. Butterfield.[7] By the end of the *Scrutiny* years,
and at the time of Leavis's maximum influence on university and
school teaching of literature in Britain, the *Scrutiny* critics believed,
with some reason, that they had had the best of the argument. But
this impression proved largely illusory in so far as longer term
impact is concerned. The influence of the *Scrutiny* conception has
waned since the early sixties while the impact of Marxian analysis
has increased. As it happened, the Hungarian uprising of 1956
spelled the effective demise not of Marxism but of vulgar Marxism
closely linked to the Communist Party. Since then the essential
impact of a sophisticated Marxism has increasingly moved into the
mainstream of all cultural disciplines including literary criticism.
This is not just a matter of committedly Marxist analysts writing
in a range of fields, it is the pervasive impact of Marxian modes of
thought on the basic terms and assumptions of the common discourse. Marxian perceptions have entered the general fabric of
intellectual life much as broadly Freudian conceptions of the
psyche and of human behaviour have done.

Now the issue essentially at stake in the dialogue with the
Marxist contributors in *Scrutiny* was the nature of human values.
The Marxist tradition had recognised that 'human values' are to a
large extent cultural products rather than manifestations of an
intrinsic human 'nature'. And since the governing assumptions
about what is 'natural' or 'human' in a culture tend to favour the
dominant interests in the given society, the Marxist critique looks
with suspicion on any appeal to intrinsic values or to an essential
humanity. Leavis, of course, accepted that our values are historically conditioned; the whole thrust of his own historical
analysis was predicated on that recognition. And what has just
been said about his way of understanding poetry suggests that his
position in practice is more phenomenological than essentialist.
That is to say he emphasises the way in which the poetically
experienced value comes to exist in the poem rather than appeal to
its existence as an *a priori* given. His opposition to the Marxist
analysis, therefore, was not in the name of a naïvely universalist
conception of values but rather from his belief that culture is an
active and positive achievement of the community in question and
embodied above all in its language.

In the abstract it might seem that the differences here are a
matter of degree. To an extent, perhaps, they are and hence the
optimistic embarking on a dialogue. Yet they reflect a major
difference in political perceptions and priorities and hence the

abortive outcome of the dialogue. Francis Mulhern in his excellent study of Leavis and *Scrutiny* argues that the Left has been too precipitate in writing him off; it would be better to accommodate, if possible, the truths he represents. And taking a longer historical view, we might note the comments of E. P. Thompson that the tradition of political radicalism and the romantic critique of industrialism in the nineteenth century were rarely able to combine.[8] In the twentieth-century version of this separation, re-enacted both in the pages of *Scrutiny* and since, we can see the reason for the mutual opposition and it is a theme to be treated at several later points in this study. At present I wish simply to note how Leavis's insistence on the irreducibility of fundamental values continues to point up an area of difficulty in the existential premises of the Marxian critical enterprise.

The impact of Marxist analysis has been to shift, I would have thought irrevocably, the fundamental assumptions of all cultural criticism. Sophisticated citizens of the late twentieth century will look on any appeal to a universal human nature with an almost reflex suspicion. As part of the general modern recognition of the latency and deviousness of human meaning (a recognition also furthered by psychoanalytic and linguistic enquiry) this is an undoubted gain. It extends the possibilities of the examined life and the means of changing cultural structures. The successful resurgence of feminist critique, for example, has been largely enabled by these modes of analysis. Yet the exercise of such diagnostic critiques is in itself an existential commitment. To a considerable extent this is a self-evident and conscious commitment which acquires its practical justification in the nature and force of the critique as exercised. But a danger lies in the assumption that this existential commitment, because it is ideologically informed, is somehow a privileged one; that it is more historically impersonal than other people's and not therefore susceptible to the diagnostic critique it exercises on opposed standpoints. This is a large issue to which I will return having considered Leavis's practice more closely, but the general point I wish to make at this stage is that the element of personal commitment underlying the Marxist critique is no less essentially problematic than it is in Leavis. His significance lies not in any 'solution' to this but in his constant and frontal engagement with it. As I have said, although he took the view when arguing against the Marxist position that there must be some universally human values if only to base the authority of Marxism on, I would prefer to stress in his actual critical practice

22

the phenomenological irreducibility of values. In so far as he now represents the most considered and forceful version of Arnoldian humanism it will be important to see the precise nature of his challenge in this regard.

Leavis's insistence on the primordial irreducibility of value judgements also came under pressure from another major source, itself related to some strains of Marxism. This was the desire to bring a scientific spirit and method to literary criticism. In the immediate environment of Cambridge English, I. A. Richards is the best example of this tendency since he started from a standpoint close in many ways to Leavis's. Richards was a founder member of the English School and research supervisor of Queenie Roth before her marriage to Leavis. Like Leavis, he was concerned to further the close examination of literary language with a view to understanding the values and processes it embodies. But in identifying his intellectual forebear in the English tradition, Richards turned to Coleridge rather than to Arnold. Leavis, in his own essay on Coleridge, had commented on how relatively little of Coleridge's voluminous theoretical writing on literary matters there was to recommend urgently to beginning students.[9] The kind of moment he valued in Coleridge was the critical rather than theoretical perception of Shakespeare's artistic impersonality; a quality which was of crucial importance for him and for the modernist generation more generally.[10] Richards responded more positively to the speculative aspect of Coleridge and applied his own speculative bent to a characteristically twentieth-century enquiry. He sought a technical, as it were scientific, account of poetic language and structure which would encompass the realm of value embodied in poetry. Leavis was opposed not, of course, to science but to scientism, or the misapplication of scientific methods and expectations. In his view the increasing thrust of Richards's work was to obfuscate the critical function, which involves an inescapable existentialist commitment, by attempting to scientificise it. The general issue is worth pausing on because the drift of Richards's work in this respect was not isolated and it has a bearing on the assumptions underlying much modern literature as well as criticism.

The conviction that a complex of values is irreducibly embodied in the verbal formulation of a poem can be taken in at least two, quite different, ways. Leavis inspected the language of poetry very closely as the irreplaceable index of the values it presented. Yet his method is far from the meticulous, exhaustive verbal analysis of, say, Cleanth Brooks. Leavis worked by quick, exemplary demonstration in conjunction with more general attestations. The effect is to focus the reader's attention through the words without allowing them to become a self-enclosed realm of explanation. For Leavis the verbal index never became a 'verbal icon' or even a 'well-wrought urn'. There was, however, a tendency in the modernist generation to draw the further, stronger inference that if poetic language is the complete index of a complex of values then human values can be encompassed by force of craftsmanship and technique. Technique becomes effectively coterminous with significance.

This inference drew support from the emphasis on technique expressed by some of the formative writers of that generation. Of course, such writers were often expressing themselves tactically and correctively and we cannot assume that their theoretical statements are necessarily to be identified with their practice, but we can see in Joyce and Pound something of this apparent apotheosis of technique. Richards's emphasis on technique is a reflection of this aspect of the modern literary movement. Mark Schorer's essay 'Technique as discovery'[11] indicates how this passed into mainstream academic practice. Indeed, this tendency was exacerbated by the spread of institutionalised literary studies in which very often technical analysis, rather than incorporate judgement, merely provides a substitute for it. Students, after all, can be trained to recognise techniques but they have to be educated to practise criticism. Hence Leavis's insistence on the phrase 'practice in criticism' as opposed to 'practical criticism' as a way of defining the exemplary activity to be conducted with, or by, students of literature.

The particular instance of I. A. Richards brings out what was at stake in Leavis's resistance to scientism generally and an essentially similar response would apply to those later critical movements such as structuralism or deconstruction which have in much more complex and philosophical ways sought to locate literary meaning in the workings of language itself to the maximal exclusion of any humanist assumption of personal moral identity or purpose in the writer. There has grown up over the last twenty years a widespread, if variegated, orthodoxy dismissing this assumption of selfhood because of its possible implication of an individual autonomy separable from social and historical construction. The most notable expression of this is Jacques Derrida's deconstructive analysis of what he calls 'the metaphysics of presence'.[12] Such views, of course, theoretically dismantle the premisses of Leavis's practice.

The first question that arises here is comparable to that raised by much Marxist critique. Should it be understood in a compensatory or a totalising sense? Is it the dislodging and revaluation of a previously hegemonic, and hence unquestioned, set of humanist assumptions or is it offered as a complete supplanting of them? Although the difference is significant it will not necessarily be evident in the conduct of such arguments. When arguing a political or forensic case, which is what such arguments often are, one is not obliged to present a balanced view of the other side. But underlying this consideration there is a further and more intrinsic difficulty. The mode of discourse developed for a given kind of critique may have no way of articulating, or properly conceiving, the opposed possibility. That is the real difficulty as between Leavis's humanism and the range of anti-humanist critiques that have grown up since the time of his major influence. Such outlooks are too incommensurate in their fundamental terms to be weighed against each other discursively. Each will only be seen, self-fulfillingly, in the reductive, if not pre-emptive, terms of the other view. It follows that Leavis could not be defended against a critique based upon such premisses as long as these premisses are accepted as setting the agenda. Hence, if we wish to consider Leavis's humanism ultimately in comparison with such opposed conceptions it is necessary in the first instance to consider the integrity and force of his practice within its own terms and that will be the principal emphasis of the following chapters. What I believe emerges from such a study is that Leavis's practice is less vulnerable than is commonly supposed to political and philosophical critique of this kind.

In this brief account of how the Arnoldian heritage was transformed in Leavis, and of how subsequent thinking about literature has proposed radically different conceptions, it has become increasingly apparent that a particular understanding of language itself is the crucial underlying issue. While suggesting that the irreducibility of poetic utterance is a widespread feature of literary modernism, I have not wished to imply that it has the same kind of significance for all the authors mentioned. Indeed, the awareness of language, and of poetic language in particular, is very varied and this points to the necessity of identifying more closely what Leavis's own conception was. In fact, his understanding of language is the crucial premiss upon which his whole view of literature, and therefore of criticism, is based. Without this, many of his statements will appear arbitrary. If his conception of language is accepted he remains, indeed, problematic but more coherently and challengingly so. I propose, therefore, to consider the question of language in some detail and then, in the following chapter, relate this in turn to his engagement with the modern movement in literature.

4
Language, Truth and Literature

I have said that Leavis's conception of literature and criticism rests upon a prior conception of language. This is the cardinal recognition upon which all Leavis's judgements and methods depend and yet hostile critics almost invariably ignore it. Indeed, the avoidance of the issue is usually so complete as to be either studied or entirely innocent. I believe the latter is predominantly the case: Leavis's conception of language has simply not impinged as an issue for critics whose own cast of mind is radically different. One reason for this can be found in the hegemony of the Saussurean tradition in modern thinking about language. Twentieth-century thought in a range of intellectual fields is characterised by a recognition of language as radically governing the ordering and understanding of experience. Leavis shared this general recognition but in a sense opposed to the philosophical and structural linguistics that evolved largely from Saussure.[1] He stressed rather the individual speakers within a speech community who provide the point of development for the language in question. The important qualities of language for him were its flexibility, its indeterminacy, its creativity and its capacity for growth as the expression of its particular culture. This emphasis on the creative processes of language does not disprove the Saussurean, and post-Saussurean, analyses so much as make them beside the point. The qualities that matter are not those that such methods can usefully discuss. But by the same token it is hard to give a systematic account of the features that Leavis regarded as cardinal and this brings us to the real difficulty for him. Any generalised, let alone a theorised, account of the workings of language in this respect would almost inevitably reduce them to banality.

27

I propose, therefore, to quote some extended extracts from his late essay 'Thought, language and objectivity' printed in *The living principle*. Most of his crucial terms and his overall conception can be found in the passages quoted. The remainder of this chapter will be devoted to a detailed examination of the meaning and adequacy of these terms. But the reader should note at once the inextricability of 'language' and 'literature' in Leavis's account. He is often accused of seeking to privilege the 'literary' over, say, the 'historical', 'scientific' or 'philosophical' domains. It should be understood that 'literary' for Leavis is certainly a necessary term but not a separable one. His concern, through literature, is for language.

> What we have to get essential recognition for is that major creative writers are concerned with a necessary kind of thought. (p. 20)

> The fundamental truth or recognition I have gestured towards, fundamental truth or recognition to which a close interrogation of experience brings us, eludes discursive treatment — a fact that doesn't prove it to be unimportant. It is when, I said, one considers one's relation to the language one was born into, and the way in which that language — in which one has vital relations with other human beings — exists, that the fundamental recognition can least be escaped, but challenges thought insistently. Where language is concerned, 'life' is human life — is man. (p. 42)

> Emphasizing the affinity between Dickens and Blake, I point out how the scheme implicit in the cast of sharply different main *personae* who interact in *Little Dorrit* applies an equivalent of Blake's distinction between the 'selfhood' and the 'identity'. Making and enforcing this point is inseparable from observing how Dickens's art insists on creativity as the characteristic of life. The selfhood asserts its rights, and possesses, from within its egocentric self-enclosure; the identity is the individual being as the focus of life — life as heuristic energy, creativity, and, from the human person's point of view, disinterestedness. It is impossible to doubt that Dickens, like Blake, saw the creativity of the artist as continuous with the general human creativity that, having created the human world we live in, keeps it renewed and real. This day-to-day work of collaborative creation includes the creating of language, without which there couldn't have been a human

world. In language, as I have said, the truth I will refer to as
'life and lives', the basic unstatable which, lost to view and left
out, disables any attempt to think radically about human life,
is most open to recognition and most invites it. In major
literary works we have the fullest use of language, and intelligent study of literature brings us inevitably to the recognition
from which, in his thinking, Andreski cuts himself off. I have
in mind, of course, the importance, and that is, the nature, of
the discipline of thought that should be associated with
'English', the university study. One can say with pregnant
brevity that the achievement of the aim in vigorous established
practice would be a potent emergence from the Cartesian
dualism. 'Potent' here means fruitful in positive consequences. A new realization of the nature and the pervasiveness
of creativity in life and thought would be fostered; there is
nothing that the world in our time more desperately needs.

The nature of livingness in human life is manifest in language
— manifest to those whose thought about language is,
inseparably, thought about literary creation. They can't but
realize more than notionally that a language is more than a
means of expression; it is the heuristic conquest won out of
representative experience, the upshot or precipitate of
immemorial human living, and embodies values, distinctions, identifications, conclusions, promptings, carto-
graphical hints and tested potentialities. It exemplifies the
truth that life is growth and growth change, and the condition
of these is continuity. It takes the individual being, the par-
ticularizing actuality of life, back to the dawn of human
consciousness, and beyond, and does this in fostering the
ahnung in him of what is not yet — the as yet unrealized, the
achieved discovery of which demands creative effort. Blake
was speaking out of the 'identity' when he said: 'Tho' I call
them Mine, I know that they are not Mine'. He was referring
to his paintings and designs, but he would have said the same
of his poems. One's criterion for calling an artist major is
whether his work prompts us to say it, emphatically and with
the profoundest conviction, for him — to put the words in his
mouth and impute to him that rare modesty which makes the
claim that is genuinely a disclaimer. (pp. 43–4)

The focal words for me at the moment are 'mean' and

'meaning'. The ease with which one shifts from one force of
the verb 'mean' to another is significant. The protest, 'Oh,
but that isn't what I mean by the word', might very well have
issued as, 'But that isn't what I meant the word to mean', or
'What I meant to mean was . . .'. There is a shift, but the
forces aren't sharply separable — there is no break, or hesita-
tion, in the continuity. It seems to me that some presence of
the force of 'intend' is necessary to the meaning of 'means'.

The full implication of this truth is sometimes slighted even
by linguistic philosophers, the reason being that it is so basic:
'the word means . . .' — the verb does its work satisfactorily
because, without thinking, they know what 'means' in the
nature of things means. But in a Wittgensteinian enterprise
such unconsciousness, intermittent and partial as it may be, is
not good enough; it produces gratuitous logic, gymnastic
fatuity, unprofitable conclusions and intellectual frustration.
Thought about language should entail the full and firm recognition that words 'mean' because individual human beings
have meant the meaning, and that there is no meaning unless
individual beings can meet in it, the completing of the
element of 'intend' being represented by the responding
someone's certitude that the last condition obtains. Individual
human beings *can* meet in a meaning because language — or
let us rather say *a* language, meaning the English language
(for there is no such thing as language in general) — is for
them in any present a living actuality that is organically one
with the 'human world' they, in growing up into it, have
naturally taken for granted. (pp. 57–8)

I first found that I needed the word 'nisus' in discussing *Ash-
Wednesday*. The problem there is to define the sense in which
the poet of 'The Hollow Men' has become religious. He will
not affirm because he cannot, not having left sufficiently
behind him the complete nihilism of that waste-land poem:
affirmation attempted merely because of the desperate intensity of his need would be empty. Will and ego (selfhood)
cannot genuinely affirm. But what he discovers or verifies in
his major poet's dealings with the English language is that
deep in him there is a Christian nisus — that is how I put it in
offering to analyse *Ash-Wednesday*, where the paradox so
manifest in the second poem — acceptance in profoundly
liturgical and biblical idiom and 'music' of death as extinction

— is representative of the whole sequence. (p. 63)

Ahnung, the other word, is intimately related — if, that is, one uses it. I myself, seeing that I had used it a number of times in writing parts of this book, cast about for an equivalent of the unnaturalizable word. I found no English substitute. Lawrence in the *Study of Thomas Hardy*, I noted, uses 'inkling' — uses it more than once. But, pondering the kind of argument for which I should want it, I decided that it hadn't enough weight — hadn't a grave enough charge of suggestiveness. 'Inkling' can translate 'Ahnung' as used in some German contexts, but it can hardly suggest anticipatory apprehension that carries the weight implicit in 'foreboding', which is often the right rendering of 'Ahnung'. (p. 63)

All writers of major creative works are driven by the need to achieve a fuller and more penetrating consciousness of that to which we belong, or of the 'Something other than itself' on which the 'physical world ultimately depends'. It is inseparable from the need to strengthen the human grasp of a significance to be apprehended in life that will inform and guide creativity. The English language in the full sense is alive, or becomes for the creative writer alive, with hints, apprehensions and intuitions. They go back to earlier cultural phases. The writer is alive in his own time, and the character of his response, the selective individual nature of his creative receptivity, will be determined by his sense — intensely individual — of the modern human condition.

He needs all the resources of the language his growing command of his theme can make spontaneous — can recruit towards the achieving of an organic wholeness: his theme itself is (being inescapably a prompting) an effort to develop, in realizing and presenting it, living continuity. The less he has to ignore or play down in achieving his 'heuristic conquest' out of representative human experience, the better — if we judge by the major artist's implicit intention. (p. 68)

The 'living intuitive faculty' is at the root of the living principle', and is felt to be strongly there in that English language in terms of which the writer lives his creative life. The 'living principle' itself is an apprehended totality of what, as registered in the language, has been won or established in immemorial human living. I say, 'an apprehended totality', for, in the nature of things, there can be no one total upshot; for every major writer it is different — there are many potentialities and no statistically determinable values. We call a writer major when we judge that his wisdom, more deeply and robustly rooted, represents a more securely poised resultant, one more fully comprehensive and humanly better centred — considerations bearing crucially on future growth — than any that any ordinarily brilliant person could offer us.

Wisdom we may call a higher plausibility, profoundly judicious and responsible. For in this realm of thought there is nothing certain or provable, and no finality. (pp. 68 – 9)

These passages contain the essential gist of the Leavisian conception and would stand without further commentary. Yet apart from the observable fact that his conception has been repeatedly ignored or misunderstood, it is evident even from the extracts themselves why that might have been so. As it happens they occur within a longish essay which begins by tracing the history of the Cambridge English faculty and makes its case by exemplary reference to specific authors. Yet even when he attempts to deal more directly with the nature of language we can see how his favoured terms such as 'life', 'potent', 'realization', 'creativity', 'responsible' and 'living intuitive faculty' would strike many readers as obscurantist asseverations; their very insistence reflecting an unadmitted vacuity at the core. Part of Leavis's difficulty arises from his avoidance of a philosopher's, or a linguistician's, vocabulary; an avoidance which clearly constitutes a challenge to the habitual premisses of both fields. And this leads him to a peculiar self-consciousness with respect to his own discourse as in his discussion of 'nisus' and '*ahnung*'. Indeed, there are many moments in his late prose where the style is denser than the matter seems to require. Yet, I believe there is an important recognition at stake for which Leavis was the pre-eminent, if not unique, spokesman. His sense of language not only explains his particular critical judgements but overrides them in importance. Or at least, I find myself dissenting from many of his particular judgements while remaining convinced by his fundamental understanding of language. I will, therefore, consider in turn the three aspects I have already implicitly distinguished: the critic as 'anti-philosopher'; the critic as philosopher; and the critic's own language.

32

The critic as anti-philosopher

Leavis's quarrel with 'philosophy' was that it was unable to provide an account of his experience of language and indeed depended on a kind of principled unawareness of this. In his view, philosophers were constitutionally 'weak on language'. The critic's holistic concern with actual uses of language involved, in Leavis's view, a more complete understanding of its nature. Now we must allow in this for Leavis's radical lack of interest in philosophy, a topic to which I will return in the course of this study, but that does not entirely remove the territorial question he raised. His refusal to be 'philosophical' was a philosophical claim and it is necessary to assess it in that light.

Leavis's belief that academic philosophy could not essentially help his own preoccupation with language was focused most clearly, perhaps, by his relations with Wittgenstein; a matter on which he has left his own record.[2] What emerges from Leavis's account is the mutual incomprehension of two personalities epitomising and reinforcing the felt gap between critic and philosopher. But the degree of mutual interest that brought them into repeated contact in Cambridge has a teasing suggestiveness about it. One of the central preoccupations of Wittgenstein's evolving account of language is the recognition of its limits. His early work, the *Tractatus logico-philosophicus* (trans. 1922), concludes: 'Of what we cannot speak, we must remain silent.' Coming as the culminating statement of the work, this dictum implies that much traditional metaphysical speculation is not so much false as meaningless. But it is a philosophical statement concerned with what philosophy as such can claim to encompass. It is not a proscription of the pragmatic and ethical usages that constitute much of ordinary parlance. In this respect Wittgenstein's dictum did not deny the importance of poetry or criticism but its concern with defining the proper scope of philosophical activity left it at best neutral with respect to how, or indeed whether, they should be conducted.

Leavis's concern with language was as radical as the early Wittgenstein's but quite different in kind. His constant critical frequentation of specific, highly individual and purposeful utterances such as poems made him deeply aware of the delicacy with which language in fact accommodates experience. Even more crucially, perhaps, new or special experiences can be expressed for which poems and scientific discoveries might be the paradigm cases. Language is always expanding and modifying. This is not just in 'response' to new circumstances or knowledge, for language is itself the medium in which new possibilities occur. Leavis understood language to be 'creative' in its capacity to generate new recognitions which may themselves then become part of the language. Since this occurs by dispersed, local and unpredictable acts, it will not readily strike the attention of an observer focused on the already existing structures and terms of the language. To consider speech acts as general phenomena is to miss the particularity of the creative moment. For Leavis, this creative penumbra around the definable body of the language was not its mere epiphenomenon, it was precisely what language was there *for*. It should be said that Wittgenstein grew much closer to this area of consideration in his later thinking which he was conducting in Cambridge at the time of his acquaintance with Leavis. He considerably modified his earlier position and was now more concerned with the ways in which communication, expression and knowledge do occur through the use of language even though they cannot be accounted for within it. Hence his adducing of what he called 'forms of life' which necessarily underlie language but are not directly expressible in it: 'to imagine a language means to imagine a form of life'.[3]

In the abstract, Wittgenstein's stringent awareness of the rational limits of language coupled with his increasing recognition of its enigmatic nature might have provided a basis on which to elaborate Leavis's counter emphasis on its astonishing expressive capacity. Both had a sense of wonder about the phenomenon of language and could step outside the framework of habit to consider its workings. And their mutual interest in the subliminal working of the common tongue is suggested in Wittgenstein's later remark: 'It is what human beings *say* that is true or false; and they agree in the *language* they use. That is not agreement in opinions but in form of life' (*Philosophical investigations*, p. 88). This is the tacit dimension to which Leavis is referring in his discussion of the word 'mean'. Hence there is a sense of potentially important unfinished business in their intellectual non-relationship. At the same time it is comprehensible enough. For even in this later phase it seems unlikely that Leavis could have gained much from Wittgenstein even had he been, as he confessedly was not, inward with Wittgenstein's mode of thinking. Wittgenstein's tendency to polarise the propositional and the enigmatic missed precisely that sense of significant and purposeful indeterminacy in which Leavis saw the

34

characteristic value of language.[4] Wittgenstein would have given him only, as it were, a negative and outer frame of reference for his concern with the creative dimension of language. As it happened, the manifest genius of Wittgenstein in his own sphere gave a clinching force to Leavis's belief that this sphere was not one that could sustain or clarify his own concerns. And the subsequent preoccupations of British philosophy in linguistic analysis and logical positivism, as in A. J. Ayer's *Language, truth and logic* (1936), would have given him no reason to change his mind.

The critic as philosopher

Tactically, then, Leavis insisted on the difference between the critic's and the philosopher's interest in language. But, as his remarks on the 'Wittgensteinian enterprise' indicate, there was lurking within this a stronger claim that criticism enforces recognitions which, in fact, are just as essential to philosophical enquiry. This is the claim that needs to be considered more closely. It is in some sense a philosophical claim. In this respect, of course, his eschewing of a philosophical vocabulary leaves him peculiarly vulnerable if indeed the criterion is one of translatability into such a vocabulary. But it would not, I think, be fruitful to attempt such a translation directly. It is more to the point that the larger philosophical tradition in Leavis's own time had sought to express a comparable view although Leavis seems to have been unaware of this. To understand Leavis, or the significance of Leavis, we need to see him not just as the inheritor of the Arnoldian critical endeavour but also as the English equivalent of the continental phenomenological tradition. For the interest of his case lies both in his similarity and in his difference from his principal continental counterparts.

Before considering this comparison more closely it should be remarked that, while German tradition provides the classic expression in Martin Heidegger and the French have a major exponent in Merleau-Ponty, it is hard to think of an equivalent American figure of comparable stature. Americans seem often to be puzzled, not by Leavis himself, but by the aura of controversy surrounding such a transparent critic. Noting the inevitable class overtones of the controversy, they might well attribute the whole fuss to the endemic British disease. But the transparency of Leavis is actually an achieved quality and its significance lies in a considered view of how readers or writers should properly inhabit language. Perhaps one reason for the unproblematic response of most Americans, whether favourable or unfavourable, lies in the relative absence in American life of those concerns by which the meaning of what he had to say could come into view at all. To be sure, the self-evident and professed Englishness of Leavis points to the local particularity of his case, but properly understood it also expresses his cousinship to a broader phenomenological tradition in which the native language has a peculiarly heightened significance.

As several commentators have observed, the nearest philosophical model for Leavis's conception of language is provided by Martin Heidegger.[5] Whereas the non-relationship of Leavis and Wittgenstein leaves an ambiguity as to whether the gap lay mainly in the personalities or in the fields of enquiry, Heidegger combines a view of language strikingly similar to Leavis's with a major philosophical intelligence. The parallels between Heidgger and Leavis have not been traced in detail which is understandable in that any reader already familiar with both writers would recognise the general affinity, and Heidegger's philosophy, or his mode of thinking on philosophical issues, is peculiarly resistant to summary statement or paraphrase. But since our present purpose is to see what Leavis's vision of language might look like if it were to be philosophically grounded, the Heideggerian parallel is invaluable.

Now Heidegger is himself a controversial figure and I do not adduce him to 'prove' Leavis to be 'right'. The point is rather that he offers a classic view and a permanent point of reference for any rival conception to take account of. Spelling out the Leavisian affinities helps to focus the same significance in Leavis. And in this connection the resistance of Heidegger to summary or paraphrase is in itself a cardinal point of parallel with Leavis. Like Leavis, Heidegger gives us not so much a 'model' of language as a sharply focused awareness of it in the light of particular questions and demands. Part of understanding his conception is to see how it must elude even his analysis although he does not, like Leavis, take this to mean that his interest is therefore unphilosophical. Like Wittgenstein, he is anti-metaphysical for an important philosophical purpose; which suggests incidentally that Leavis may have sold his own position short by his rejection of 'philosophy'. I propose, therefore, to enumerate some of the pertinent Heideggerian themes and insights using very largely direct quotations from Heidegger's later essays on art, poetry and language to bring out the implicit complexity of thought in Leavis.[6] For Heidegger attempts to formulate in philosophical terms recognitions which, even in Leavis's most direct statements, always depend upon a prior experience of critical reading.

The similarity and difference is evident in their common concern with language as the index of an order beyond discourse. But whereas Leavis appeals to 'life' Heidegger's concern was with the nature of Being; a term usually capitalised to signal that the reference is not to some particular being but to the very fact of Being at all. In the latter part of his *œuvre* he attempted to engage this philosophical concern more concretely, if more obliquely, by considering the nature of art, poetry and language. Hence he says in reference to the essay on which I am mainly drawing here:

> The whole essay, 'The Origin of the Work of Art', deliber-
> ately yet tacitly moves on the path of the question of the
> nature of Being. Reflection on what *art* may be is completely
> and decidedly determined only in regard to the question of
> Being.[7]

As Heidegger explained at the opening of his first major work *Being and time* (1927) the traditional attempts of Western philo-sophy to understand, or to be properly conscious of, Being have in fact obscured it; they have made it metaphysical. His attempt was to recover in terms appropriate to a modern, and hence post-metaphysical, understanding something of the apprehension of Being which he saw in the pre-Socratic Greek philosophers.[8] Since our whole language is constitutively imbued with the assumptions of the Western philosophical tradition it is difficult to find any terms with which to approach Being in the right way. The impor-tance of art in this connection is that it can offer such an apprehen-sion of Being. As he says: 'The work of art opens up in its own way the Being of beings' ('Origin', p. 39).

Heidegger approaches this proposition by distinguishing the mere object, such as a stone, from an 'instrument' such as a hammer. We take objects for granted and hence pass over, or fail to attend to, their Being. In the case of instruments we rather pass through the object to respond to its use and therefore still do not respond to its Being. He then suggests that a work of art combines aspects of both: it is created, just as an instrument is, but like a natural object it has no ulterior purpose. This combination focuses our apprehension on its Being:

In general, of everything present to us, we can note that it *is*; but this also, if it is noted at all, is noted soon to fall into oblivion, as is the wont of everything commonplace. And what is more commonplace than this, that a being, is. In a work, by contrast, this fact, that it *is* as a work, is just what is unusual. The event of its being created does not simply reverberate through the work; rather, the work casts before itself the eventful fact that the work is as this work, and it has constantly this fact about itself. The more essentially the work opens itself, the more luminous becomes the uniqueness of the fact that it is rather than is not. ('Origin', pp. 65–6)

As one of his examples, Heidegger discusses a painting by Van Gogh of a pair of peasant shoes and here it becomes necessary for us to distinguish what he means by Being from a neutral existence. Since we have consciousness, we experience Being within a 'world' of significances rather than as a neutral 'earth'. I express it in this way for purposes of exposition in a familiar language although Heidegger would avoid terms such as 'we' or 'consciousness' because of their implied, metaphysical separation of mind and world. His use of 'world' is meant to deny the possibility of this separation which our language constantly imposes on us. Hence the Being of the peasant shoes is not a mere existence but is grounded in, and therefore expresses, the world of their use; the world of the peasant woman. The expression of Being in a work of art, therefore, is not essentially contingent on a representional or mimetic conception. Being is expressed in the bodying forth of the 'world' of the object rather than in its sheer fact as an 'earthly' existent. Heidegger's use of 'world', translated in Sartre as *'la réalité humaine'*, is designed to break down the Cartesian dualism of 'consciousness' and world. This anti-Cartesianism is equally fundamental to Leavis. There is obviously a related intention in Leavis's phrase 'human world' which is repeated and then placed in quotation marks over the course of the quoted extracts. Heidegger's usage, along with his whole style, seeks to alienate the word from its ordinary use and enforce its special meaning. Leavis typically wishes to remain within accepted usage while highlighting the special force he wishes the phrase to have.

This conception of a 'world' is crucial to Heidegger's understanding of Being and it underwrites, as with Leavis too, the nature of his concern with language. For the above remarks on art in general do not just include poetry. Poetry is singled out as the privileged instance of art because it has language as its medium. Language is the modality in which Being in a 'world', as opposed to mere existence on the earth, is possible.

> To see this, only the right concept of language is needed. In the current view, language is held to be a kind of communication. It serves for verbal exchange and agreement, and in general for communicating. But language is not only and not primarily an audible and written expression of what is to be communicated. It not only puts forth in words and statements what is overtly or covertly intended to be communicated; language alone brings what is, as something that is, in to the Open for the first time. Where there is no language, as in the being of plant, stone or animal, there is also no openness of what is, . . . ('Origin', p. 73)

Heidegger perhaps understates the sophistication of other contemporary views of language here, but he makes clear its primordial and constitutive significance for the apprehension of Being in a 'world'. It is language that makes a 'world'. Or as Leavis says '. . . language, without which there could not have been a human world'.

Hence Heidegger came to speak of language as the 'house of Being'. Language is not Being, nor can it explain or disclose Being, but it is a condition of Being and contemplation of language helps in its apprehension. Like Wittgenstein, therefore, in this respect Heidegger has himself to use language to gesture towards a recognition that cannot be directly stated within it. The necessary indirectness can be seen in the very phrase 'house of Being' as he points out in 'A dialogue on language': 'Even the phrase "house of Being" does not provide a concept of the nature of language, to the great sorrow of philosophers who in their disgruntlement see in such phrases no more than a decay of thinking.'[9] Leavis's critical rhetoric has met with comparable objections and it is evident why Heidegger turned in his later years to illustration from German poetry and, as in the present instance, developed a poetic strain within his own discourse. If an anglophone reader wishes to understand demonstratively what Heidegger means by 'dwelling' in language, as opposed to mere existence on the earth, the ending of Ben Jonson's 'To Penshurst' may be helpful:

> Those proud, ambitious heaps, and nothing else,
> May say, their lords have built, but thy lord dwells.

Jonson's poem is not essentially a description of the Sidney family's estate at Penshurst. He rather creates in language, by way of a courtly compliment, a vision of its best, ideal self. That is the true 'world' of the poem. This is signalled by a note of controlled hyperbole which at the same time allows a concrete and even earthy reference to the actual: 'Fat, aged carps, that runne into thy net' (line 33). The poem moves gradually up the scale of being, in Jonson's renaissance understanding of the term, to affirm its final definition of human dwelling. The poem, of course, has a quite different philosophical conception behind it from those poems in which Heidegger seeks to indicate the dwelling of Being. But it strikingly demonstrates the constitutive function of the poem's language in creating the 'world' in which this 'dwelling' occurs.[10]

Leavis's practice rests on similar convictions to those quoted so far from Heidegger, and it is important to note that poetry in this view is not just a specialised use of language but rather its most primordial, world-creating instance. Poetry for present purposes is not to be defined by formal properties such as verse and rhyme. It is simply language in its most pregnant, authentic and creative uses although these properties will be found pre-eminently, of course, in artistic contexts. Such a view of poetry has consequences for what we might mean by 'thinking': a theme already touched on in the preceding chapter with respect to Leavis and modernism. As we have seen, Heidegger believed that some traditional forms of ratiocinative intellection actually obscure the nature of Being, and that 'thinking' should therefore be conditioned by the qualities of poetry. He is careful not to identify poetry with thinking, or to exalt poetry over thinking, and indeed it is important in his view that they remain distinct. And yet both poetry and thinking are fully performing their own functions only when, as he says, they 'neighbour' each other. Thinking, we might say, is reflective. Poetry, in being more primordial, works at a largely pre-reflective level. Both are necessary and each needs to recognise the other. This is the equal 'co-presence' that Leavis had in mind when seeing poetry as a 'necessary kind of thought'. Poetry is not a decorative addition to thought but is itself a radical process of thinking.

All language has a pre-reflective dimension to it. The poet is distinguished by the ability to attend to, and make positive use of, this level of language. The poet's relation to the pre-reflective is equally cardinal in Leavis's conception. On several occasions he commented approvingly on a poet's ability to prevent an incipiently formed image from being made fully explicit. And this sense of poetic language includes another aspect that has been especially, and controversially, associated with Leavis: his view that language may in some way 'enact' the experience.

Heidegger has some highly pertinent comments on the importance of the physical aspect of speech.

> Vocalization and sounds may no doubt be explained physiologically as a production of sounds. But the question remains whether the real nature of the sounds and tones of speech is ever thus experienced and kept before our eyes. We are instead referred to melody and rhythm in language and thus to the kinship between song and speech. All would be well if only there were not the danger of understanding melody and rhythm also from the perspective of physiology and physics, that is, technologically, calculatingly in the widest sense. No doubt much can be learned in this way that is correct, but never, presumably, what is essential. It is just as much a property of language to sound and ring and vibrate, to hover and to tremble, as it is for the spoken words of language to carry a meaning. But our experience of this property is still exceedingly clumsy, because the metaphysical-technological explanation gets everywhere in the way, and keeps us from considering the matter properly.[11]

Heidegger recognises the difficulty of talking about the expressive physicality of language. A technically descriptive accuracy in this matter is likely to miss what is essential. Our language has no term for the exercising of skill in the pre-reflective and gestural realms. Unless poetry is such a term. But language, he claims, is expressive by what it does as well as by what it says. Similarly, for Leavis this aspect of language is not an optional, and rather hypothetical, extra. It is the mode, and index, of the poet's dwelling in language. In his reading of Keats's 'Ode to Autumn', for example, this quality is of the essence.[12]

The general issue here, that language may in some sense 'enact' its meaning, has been a matter of long-standing dispute. The classic occasion in the English tradition is Dr Johnson's objection to Pope's dictum that 'The Sound must seem an Eccho to the Sense'. Pope's neo-classical formulation proposes that sound should 'echo' the sense rather than make the post-romantic claim that it should 'enact' it. Yet even this comparatively modest claim

Johnson sought to refute by adducing as a counter-instance two alternative meanings for a given rhythm.[13] What this exchange brings out is not that Pope or Johnson is wrong but that they are both right from their respective viewpoints. Johnson is 'correct' (to borrow Heidegger's term) in insisting, for the sake of clear thinking, that the sound has no intrinsic meaning; it is not in fact an echo of the sense. But, of course, Pope did not claim that it was; only that it should 'seem' so. And indeed Pope's practice indicates that he was fully alive to the force of this distinction as in his lines:

> Yet ne'er one sprig of Laurel graced these ribalds,
> From slashing Bentley down to pidling Tibalds.[14]

He brilliantly exploits and degrades the name Theobald by capitalising on the disjuncture between its sound and its spelling. The effect occurs between the true spelling of Theobald and the sounds of 'pidling' and 'ribald'. Pope knew as well as Shakespeare's Juliet that a rose by any other name would smell the same. He also understood that for her the name Romeo would never again be an arbitrary signifier. His function as a poet is to put a charged value into words which they do not have as they sit in the dictionary. Pope's lines bring out this principle with an exceptional clarity because of their comic incongruity; their focus on the arbitrariness of a name; and the very salient formal structure of the verse. But what they demonstrate in general is the epiphenomenal plane on which poetry can project its 'world'.

The Johnsonian point has been more recently restated by Peter Barry who cites Leavis as one of the more sophisticated critics to be caught in the enactment 'fallacy'.[15] Barry is right to insist, as a teacher of literature, that students should not make a literalistic appeal to an unreal phenomenon. But there is a qualitative difference between the literalistic understanding of enactment found in freshman essays and the subtle imaginative processes created by great poets. And the force of the difference lies also in the larger conception of language in which the act of reading is seen to take place. Leavis's way of talking about 'enactment' indicates that he understood this distinction very well. Indeed, it is worth noting that Leavis's part in the modern appreciation of Pope involved an awareness of his verbal richness and his way of dwelling in the spoken tongue while Johnson's formal principles were confessedly unable to accommodate this aspect of Shakespeare.

The Heideggerian account of language helps to define the status and significance of this enactive or embodying dimension in poetic utterance. It is not to be taken as a mystified alternative to 'ordinary' discourse. Part of its importance is precisely its continuity with the language as a whole for which it provides a creative edge. It should be seen rather as a crystallising potential of the language that can only occur at a point of controlled intensity. Its importance is that it often provides the way in to the experience whether for the poet or for the reader.[16] And the Heideggerian 'definition' should likewise prevent us from taking 'enactment' in too literalistic and imitative a sense. Certainly for Leavis any merely imitative use of sound would fall short of poetry and his discussion of poetic language always insists on its 'analogous' relation to experience. It is more to do with creating the 'world' of the experience than depicting some particular entity 'out there'. The register of language in use implied by the term 'enactment' remains elusive of generalised or analytic definition partly because it is not contingent upon a literalistic imitation. It is strictly an *effect* of the expressive context as a whole rather than a separable phenomenon that can be adduced as the expressive *cause*.

Leavis's 'enactment', then, is importantly clarified by his affinity with Heidegger. Both attribute crucial expressive value to aspects of language which, for a more instrumental view, are merely illusory. And such aspects are not just expressive, they are the medium in which the poet creatively attends. Language is the historical creation of its community and conditions pre-reflectively the nature of its particular world. As Heidegger puts it 'There is no such thing as natural language occurring of itself without a destiny. All language is historical, even where man does not know history in the modern European sense.'[17] This last statement is equally central to Leavis as in his reference to 'immemorial human living'. For him, too, language significantly precedes not only the individual but the succeeding generations of speakers so that in its 'world'-forming capacity it speaks through them in being spoken by them. There is, therefore, an impersonal dimension even in the personal act of speech. Heidegger explains how attentiveness to Being, for him, is achieved partly through attentiveness to language as it speaks:

If attention is fastened exclusively on human speech, if human speech is taken to be simply the voicing of the inner man, if speech so conceived is regarded as language itself, then the nature of language can never appear as anything but an expression and an activity of men. But human speech, as the speech of mortals, is not self-subsistent. The speech of mortals rests in its relation to the speaking of language.[18]

And he moves to the conclusion of this essay reinforcing his emphasis by the paragraphing:

> Language speaks.
> Man speaks in that he responds to language. This responding is a hearing. It hears because it listens to the command of stillness.
> It is not a matter here of stating a new view of language.
> What is important is learning to live in the speaking of language. ('Language', p. 210)

Again the last sentence is particularly significant for Leavis despite its remoteness from his idiom. His resistance to elaborating his own view of language in a conceptual way arose in part from his awareness that there was nothing new, at that level, for him to say. Yet his critical endeavour might well be seen as a 'learning to live in the speaking of language'. Furthermore, Leavis's remarks on the 'disinterestedness' of the great artist, a quality he found encapsulated in Blake's distinction between 'identity' and 'self-hood', indicate why 'impersonality' is such a crucial term for him. The comparison with Heidegger brings out how this is more than a personal moral achievement; it is what gives the artist's use of the common tongue its 'philosophical' value. Where literary art is in question, such an impersonality may be defined as the speaker's relation to language. The great poet is able to 'listen' to the language. The serious reader or critic may attempt, perhaps, to overhear.

For both Heidegger and Leavis this sense of utterance as an interplay between the personal and the impersonal dimensions of the language helps explain its creative aspect. Heidegger called this the 'projective' and associated it particularly with poetry:

> Projective saying is saying which, in preparing the sayable, simultaneously brings the unsayable as such into a world. In such saying, the concepts of an historical people's nature, i.e., of its belonging to world history, are formed for that folk, before it. ('Origin', p. 74)

The individual act of creation, that is to say, arises in part from attentiveness to language and once it is achieved it in turn expands and modifies the capacity of that language. Again, this is not a new conception. Heidegger, indeed, quotes W. von Humboldt making the same point in the early nineteenth century, but as he says of Humboldt's comment it is one 'whose adequate interpretation would require a separate study' ('The way to language', p. 18). It is a matter rather of recognising the significance of the abstractly stated point and Heidegger's idiosyncratic style, like Leavis's assertive intensity, is the attempt not so much to explain an idea as to bring home a recognition. Heidegger's 'projective' has its equivalent in Leavis's 'nisus' and '*ahnung*' where, as usual, he has to explain the meaning by dwelling on the inadequacy of the terms.

Perhaps part of the difficulty here is that an ambitious claim for language as a whole can only be demonstratively vindicated in supreme, and therefore special, instances. Of course, both Heidegger and Leavis recognise well enough that language exists much of the time in corrupted and decadent forms with only rare manifestations of its true capacity. This brings us to the single most controversial aspect of Leavis and the one for which the Heideggerian parallel is most illuminating. In noting the impersonality of great art, Heidegger remarks parenthetically that for his present analysis only great art is in question. 'It is precisely in great art — and only great art is in question here — that the artist remains inconsequential as compared with the work, almost like a passageway that destroys itself in the creative process for the work to emerge' ('Origin', p. 40). While this sentence bears generally on the Leavisian theme of creative impersonality, its parenthesis points towards the vexed question of his 'narrowness' of taste and judgement. For, like Heidegger, Leavis believed that great literature has a representative value to be explained not just in terms of the artist's 'experience' but in terms of its profound relation to the common tongue; its ability to touch the primordial linguistic bases of experience. More will need to be said on the issue of Leavis's narrowness in the light of specific cases, but it should be noted that for both Heidegger and Leavis the weightiness of the central claim has a built-in exclusiveness. The parenthetical nature of Heidegger's comment reflects its following so naturally from the overall view he has expounded. But Leavis's exclusiveness, his continual meditation on major works, has been seen as merely perverse and temperamental. His insistence on

. . identifying the canon of 'major' writers at the expense of 'minor' ones did not mean that he had only read the major ones. And there were tactical and pedagogical considerations behind this insistence; his criticism was always a larger aspect of his teaching. But the comparison with Heidegger focuses a more fundamental reason for his emphasis. The kind of value that was at stake for him in literature was only to be found in works of a certain order. He had not the catholicity of many literary persons because his ultimate interest, one might say, was not in literature but in what literature could reveal or create. This concern gave a unique irradiation to his reading and exclusiveness is its necessary condition. Moreover, Leavis's exclusiveness merely highlights, it does not create, the problem. The force of this point may be seen by comparing Raymond Williams's remarks in *The long revolution*. He comments that it is a difficulty in 'aesthetic theory' that great art and the latest cheap novel are 'the result of the same general activity'.[19] Quite so, Leavis might reply.

But the difficulty of demonstrating such representative value is real and it is part of the general difficulty of affirming significance at all. Indeed, the tendency of this comparison with Heidegger has been increasingly to throw attention back from the definition of art to the practice and rhetoric of criticism. To conclude this comparison, therefore, I will comment on two further aspects of Leavis's critical practice for which Heidegger offers some explicitly methodological pointers. These arise from the way Heidegger's account of art as a bringing of Being into presence is careful not to imply a disclosing of Being in the sense of explaining it. As he says in his epilogue to 'The origin of the work of art', art remains a 'riddle' and his reflections in the essay 'are far from claiming to solve the riddle. The task is to see the riddle' ('Origin', p. 79). Art remains a riddle partly because what it brings into presence is not in itself explicable. Leavis, of course, has a different sense of what poetic art presents; 'life' is a different term from 'Being'. But given his own conviction of the irreducibility of literary utterance, as already noted, he shows a comparable chastity with respect to any claims to explain it. The critical language is to be both ambitious and modest. Part of the discipline of criticism lies in recognising its limits.

That is the light in which to consider the following, rather more opaque, comment by Heidegger:

The preservers of a work belong to its createdness with an

essentiality equal to that of its creators. But it is the work that makes the creators possible in their nature, and that by its own nature is in need of preservers. If art is the origin of the work, the creator and the preserver, originate, each in his own nature. ('Origin', p. 71)

Some of the difficulty of this passage arises from its specific context and I am not concerned to explain it in detail. What is to be noted is the way Heidegger accords to the preserver, or reader in the case of literature, an equal 'essentiality'. The reader does not create the work yet may 'belong to its createdness'. This points to an aspect of critical reading which Leavis does not emphasise as an abstract claim but which is everywhere implied in the practice of his criticism. A fully engaged reading of literature, like musical performance, is a creative act even though performed within the terms of the given work. Or, we might say, the act of reading may be of a secondary order but it attains the status of criticism only when it is as primary as the act of composition; when it can lend both weight and a counterweight to the original. As an idea this is just as problematic as Heidegger's image of the 'house of Being'. But Heidegger's other image of 'listening' to the language may be extended to indicate the peculiar intensity of Leavisian reading. Leavis tries to listen not just to what the poet says but to what the poet has 'heard' in order to say it. Leavis characteristically participates, as a reader, not just in the completed work so much as in the implied activity of its composition. This also reflects on the issue of intensity and narrowness. Without supposing that he could have written the work in question, it is as if Leavis needed to identify imaginatively with the impulse to write it. The emphasis on identification here, which of course denotes an identification with the process enacted in the language rather than emotional identification with a character or an author, indicates how Leavis's gestures towards analysis should be understood. They are not attempts to 'explain' the text so much as a quasi-musical notation for the inward performance that Leavis has in mind by the act of 'reading'. He attempts to bring the text 'off the page', as in a *viva voce* reading, while preserving the linguistic, rather than literalistic, nature of the poetic experience.

We might say that the *enactive* aspect of poetic language has its counterpart in the *participatory* dimension of reading; without appealing in either case to a literalistically mimetic conception. There is, of course, more to be said about both poetic language

47

and critical discourse but the constitutive importance of these elements characterises the Leavisian practice. If they are not the whole, they are close to the heart, of the matter. That is to speak metaphorically but not, if Heidegger's example can be appealed to, meaninglessly about Leavis's readerly relation to the work. But it is also desirable to make more analytic sense of his readerly practice and Heidegger's second methodological pointer touches classically on a further objection commonly made to Leavis.

In stressing the mutuality of 'creators' and 'preservers' Heidegger incidentally highlights the characteristic predicament of all interpretative and critical discourse: its circular relation to its text. In the hermeneutical tradition (the methodological study of textual interpretation) the process of interpretation has often been characterised as a circle. A particular detail of a text cannot be understood until there is a sense of the whole, yet equally the whole cannot be understood without the parts. Hence, it is argued, there must be a pre-understanding which is taken to the text. Logically the process dissolves into a vicious circle. Yet empirically it appears to yield results. Ideally, it should be a process of discovery whereby the traffic between the text and its interpretative model is mutually modifying. Since the matter of circularity has frequently been raised as an objection to Leavis it is helpful to note a comment of Heidegger in one of his later pieces, 'A dialogue on language', in which he casts himself as the Inquirer in dialogue with a Japanese colleague.

> *Japanese.* Did you not say earlier that this circle is inevitable, and that, instead of trying to avoid it as an alleged logical contradiction, we must follow it?
> *Inquirer.* Yes. But this necessary acceptance of the hermeneutic circle does not mean that the notion of the accepted circle gives us an originary experience of the hermeneutical relation.
> *Japanese.* In short, you would abandon your earlier view.
> *Inquirer.* Quite — and in this respect, that talk of a circle always remains superficial.

> ('Dialogue', p. 51)

This comment by the later Heidegger recognises the inevitability of a circular structure in a certain kind of argument while insisting that the mere fact of the circularity does not reflect on the quality of the argument. In Leavis's case the issue of circularity has been especially salient because his characteristic concern is not even interpretative. His characteristic endeavour is not to disclose meaning as something that needs unravelling: it is to give an adequacy of attention to the self-evident. Self-evidence raises an even more serious, potentially stultifying, circularity. It remains to be seen how Leavis deals with this, but it is worth noting in the light of Heidegger's remarks here, that the circularity which would be damaging in logical contexts may not be so in a context, such as a meditative one, in which the purpose is a gathering of attention. Leavis's critical practice is very different from Heidegger's philosophical meditation on literary texts but their common problem of revealing the self-evident makes Heidegger's explicit attention to his own discourse a pertinent analogy for Leavis's implicit procedures.

I have given considerable space to Heidegger's conception of language since it has so many points of affinity with Leavis's and it will therefore continue to provide a focus of principle for the closer analysis of Leavis's practice in the following chapters. But it must always be understood that Heidegger's primary interest is philosophical even when he is discussing literary texts. Hence, there is a contemplative, or speculative, cast to his focus on language and, in keeping with this, the poetic works to which he appeals have for the most part a thematic consciousness of language or Being in something like the Heideggerian sense. Indeed, despite Heidegger's opposition to the traditional category of the 'aesthetic' because of its overtones of connoisseurship and its grounding in metaphysics, his own account of the art work, using the distinction between object and instrument, rests on a non-instrumental instrumentality comparable to Kant's definition of the aesthetic as 'purposiveness without purpose'. He is attempting to define the nature of art in principle and the magisterial weight of his account derives from its universality. Leavis, by contrast, is concerned with specific emotional quality and value. His conception of language is manifest in his way of responding to its local and varied uses. As a critic, he has very different purposes and in noting their affinity with respect to language I am not seeking to enlist him as an unwitting Heideggerian. The positive point of the comparison is to emphasise that one cannot begin to appreciate the force and logic of Leavis's criticism unless it is seen to be resting on a coherent equivalent, within its own native tradition, for continental phenomenology. That does not prove him 'right'; it only pushes the problem a stage further back. But it pushes it back to where it belongs and make it properly visible. He is likely to appear naïve or inconsistent if translated into any neo-Cartesian terms. His endeavour, like Heidegger's, was to challenge such terms root and branch.

It has become evident from these remarks on Wittgenstein and Heidegger that if one seeks philosophical models for Leavis's understanding of language, the philosophers concerned will be those either beating the bounds of language or straining to reach beyond them. To put the matter in this way suggests the two complementary impulses that between them span modern consciousness of language: on the one hand a radical awareness of its delusive and distorting nature and on the other hand a belief in its truth-telling and expressive capacity. These two aspects are the poles between which the creative use of language, in Leavis's understanding, must occur. The significant 'truths' of great art are won as on a high wire over an abyss. Great art, within this conception, is likely not just to fail, but to lapse into sentimental falsity and delusion. Leavis's dwelling on failed artistry, even in the writers he admires, is intrinsic to his understanding of positive achievement. This dual recognition can be seen in other 'philosophical' accounts of language which highlight the difference between Leavis's concerns and Heidegger's.

· The negative recognition was given memorable expression by Nietzsche in his early essay 'On truth and falsehood in their extra-moral sense'.[20] Truth, he said, 'is a mobile army of metaphors'. In distinguishing metaphor as a special figure of speech we posit a secure point of reference in the literal. But the distinction, Nietzsche pointed out, is quite relative. All language and thinking are, or have grown from, the metaphorical. The naturalising of metaphor into the apparently literal is a delusion; and a dangerous one in so far as it remains unrecognised. Language permits no unmediated vision. It is fraught with governing structures which we cannot, as beings thinking in language, step behind to assess. As he remarked later, we think we have got rid of God yet still believe in grammar. But the analytic recognitions underlying this radical suspicion of language can be given a highly positive implication. The later works of Paul Ricoeur, notably *The rule of metaphor*,[21] are a striking example of this.

Ricoeur also starts by focusing on the trope of metaphor. But he argues that metaphor, which conflates two known objects to create what is essentially a new one, epitomises the creative activity of the mind in language. And far from being an isolated trope, as traditional rhetoric has supposed, a metaphor can only come into being by drawing on the possibilities latent in its context and indeed in the language at large. To use a time-honoured metaphor, this apparently separable and ornamental feature is in fact the tip of the linguistic iceberg. Also, as Aristotle observed, metaphor is the element of natural genius in the writing of poetry: it is a function of intuitive perception and cannot be taught. If we put these considerations together, Ricoeur argues, the specialness of metaphor, far from making it isolable and ornamental *vis-à-vis* 'normal' usage, makes it the type case of human creativity as enabled by language in all fields of enquiry. Metaphor in this view is the heuristic edge of language. The edge of a blade is where it tapers into non-existence yet the whole meaning of a knife is gathered at that point. And 'dead' metaphors, rather than being merely a sign of exhaustion or the distortion of some literal meaning, are part of the process of growth and change. Dead metaphors must once have been alive and they have given that life to the language. They are the leaf mould which sustains, as it returns to the parent body, the new points of growth. These organic metaphors are, of course, my own not Ricoeur's but they reflect the spirit suggested by his original French title *La Métaphore vive*.

Ricoeur is useful to the present discussion because his theoretical account enables us to see its accommodation of the counter-conception. He is not merely giving a positive value to metaphor but grounds this in an overall conception of language analytically cognate with the deconstructive critique, as we might now call it, of Nietzsche's early essay. It is also useful in that just as Heidegger helps define the implications of 'enactment' in poetry, so Ricoeur develops a more closely theorised account than Heidegger of what Leavis means by 'creativity'. Indeed, it is indicative that in expounding his case Ricoeur has drawn extensively on Anglo-American literary theory. But it is equally indicative, in that connection, that he has drawn on literary theory, not criticism. *The rule of metaphor* is argued in purely theoretical terms and adduces virtually no examples of metaphor whether in poetry or in common usage. Actually, Leavis's practical demonstrations of creativity in language are the precise equivalent of the recognitions that Ricoeur is reaching by a theoretical route. Once again it is a striking instance of the *de facto* separation of the philosophical, or at least the theoretical, and the critical realms. Leavis may be guilty of acquiescing too readily in this but he did not invent it. For

Ricoeur's argument is not really in parallel with Leavis in the sense that, had these works been written earlier, Leavis might have found them useful. Ricoeur has rather constructed a lengthy theoretical case whose terminus *is* Leavis's experiential premiss and starting-point: the manifest *fact* of creativity in language.

Comparing Ricoeur and the early Nietzsche in this way indicates how sharp oppositions of attitude do not necessarily imply a black and white opposition in the analyses. Even while the one attitude is being expressed it has in fact to accommodate the opposite recognition. Nietzsche who distrusted language so radically is yet one of the consummate masters of expression in German even in the act of saying so. And Ricoeur's positive conception of metaphor rests on the radical instability of language and meaning. This focus on attitude as an existential choice to some extent distinguishable from the analysis is important to the understanding of what Leavis means by criticism. For in Leavis's view the critic's sensitivity to language must encompass both dimensions: its dangers and its creative capacity; although the critic will naturally engage these in literary rather than philosophical terms. And if it is indeed the case that analysis may subserve, but not of itself enforce, a particular attitude then we can say that Leavis is going for the nub of the matter by eschewing an analytic account of language for a critical assessment of its use on particular occasions. He seeks to maintain a sense of language as the arena of total potentiality rather than offer a totalised 'view' of language as such. Or in his own words 'I say, "an apprehended totality" for, in the nature of things, there can be no one total upshot; for every writer is different —.' Hence he himself was acutely sensitive to the twin possibilities just discussed, the delusive and the creative capacities of language, and he was strongly aware, as was Heidegger, that language can only be spoken by an individual yet is the possession of an historical community. There is a sense in which language can never be 'purely individual'. And by the same token the individual is implicated, whether knowingly or nor, in the life of the language at large. But all these recognitions manifest themselves by an inward focus of attention on the specific use of language; an attention for which we can best use the word 'responsibility'.

This is the standpoint from which to consider his detestation, the word is not too strong, of whatever he considered as irresponsibility in language. Language is not just the 'expression' of ideas and feelings, it is the index, and means, of our grasp on experience both individually and communally. Utterance is an enactment of moral identity albeit much of the time in a neutral or potential manner. Since the individual speaker draws, in a largely sub-liminal way, on the communal resource of language, this will always provide a potential momentum on which the speaker, and the audience, can be carried. Hence where the speaker is not taking full responsibility, the conventional habits of feeling, as well as 'thought', will assert themselves; and the most likely manifesta-tion of this is as a comforting sense of personal thought and first-hand response. Indeed, the logic of this principle may apply even more strongly to social or ideological sub-groupings whose conscious purpose is to challenge 'conventional' assumptions as perceived in the culture at large. Leavis's characteristic point of critique is not an assumption or belief *per se* but the quality of self-awareness with which it is understood. The deconstructive recognition in recent French theory that the individual is often 'spoken' by the language rather than vice versa has a pragmatic parallel in Leavis's critical vigilance with respect to language. This is not to equate them, of course. Leavis's vigilance does not neces-sarily give him the specifically ideological purchase on others or himself which deconstructive critiques seek to achieve. He differs from the Derridean analysis, and indeed from Heidegger's, in that his attention is on the awareness and integrity of the speaker, or writer, as the focus of responsibility. At the same time, as has often been noted, there remains a potentially disabling paradox for whatever deconstructive agency conducts the theoretical dis-mantling of the 'metaphysics of presence'. As soon as a decon-structive analysis is put to use then the issue of the responsible self must arise.

With his concentration on the elements of feeling and self-image, rather than ideological structures, Leavis is aware less of deception, perhaps, than of seduction. The blurring and seductive aspects of language may be even more potent and harder to identify than ideological premisses which can be analytically fore-grounded. His hostility to the 'musical' tradition in English verse from Spenser to Tennyson arose from his suspicion of its emotional undertow even in such a distinguished practitioner as he recognised Tennyson to be. And a comparable seductiveness may lurk in discursive prose, including the discourse of criticism. Very often, when disagreeing with academic or journalistic opponents, it was neither the detachable opinions nor the individual personali-ties that were at issue for him so much as the whole mode of discourse in which conventional responses were reinforced by inertia. It may, indeed, have struck some readers that the passages quoted from Heidegger about 'listening' to the language could be construed in a damaging sense; particularly if one thinks of the effects of rhetorical *schwärmerei* in modern German history. It seems to me that Hitler's audiences were precisely not listening in Heidegger's sense; and nor perhaps was Heidegger on occasion. But the controversy concerning his relation to Nazism points us to the importance of the critical function which is necessary to give Heidegger's injunction its real force. Leavis's listening was always a critical listening. This point bears on Leavis's own 'political' stance. In his later years particularly he was commonly perceived as highly conservative despite his support, during most of his life, for the Liberal party. As far as I can see, his concern for continuity was complemented, as part of its inner logic, by an equally strong, indeed iconoclastic, perception of the need for radical change. But his sense of what mattered for the quality of communal life left him agnostic with respect to specific political models. His concern was with the conditions in which any political activity could be significant. His position was far from a-political and could perhaps best be described as 'pre-political'.

Leavis's criticism, then, consists of a high standard of vigilance trained by attention to classic instances of language used, in the senses just indicated, both creatively and responsibly. So far, of course, I am merely indicating the general implication of these terms. An assessment of their actual value in use will be the business of the following chapters. But as we proceed to that assessment we should note that one increasing implication of this account is that the view of language underlying his reading of literature is one that especially commits him to an exemplary practice in his criticism. Much of the significance of what he says lies in the means by which he gets it said.

The critic's language

Of all the philosophical figures mentioned, it is perhaps Nietzsche who provides the most pertinent example for Leavis's own use of language. This is not to suggest a general affinity with Nietzsche either philosophically or stylistically but simply to emphasise the complex demands placed on his own mode of expression. Nietzsche's cultural critique, as has been seen, involved a

potentially disabling critique of language and of the power of
reason; the very media he was himself obliged to use. But he was
not only a deconstructor for he was also committed to the affirmation of values. In the event he communicated his existential
critique, and his affirmations, in a style that capitalised on the
uncertainties of his medium. His epigrams and ironies, his own
'mobile army' of metaphor and fable, all constitute an extraordinary demonstrative employment of language in the service of
his recognitions. Nietzsche is indeed accused on occasion of
disabling self-contradiction for making use of the very grammar
and logic he had elsewhere diagnosed as decadent symptoms. But
when, for example, he diagnoses the rise of Socratic dialectic as a
decadent symptom in the history of Greek culture, he is not
rejecting this use of reason *as such*. He is asking what motives
might underlie the development of this powerful instrument for
use in a competitive arena. His diagnosis depends precisely on its
being an authoritative means.[22] The point here is that one has to
follow the adjustments in diagnostic viewpoint rather than attach
permanent evaluative labels to single entities. Although less flam-
boyantly than in Nietzsche, Leavis's critical language requires a
comparable readiness of implicit adjustment as he moves between
planes of reference such as character, author, text and context to
build a rounded and whole apprehension of the work. When we
read Nietzsche we *know* he is making demands on our intelligence;
the implicitness of Leavis's demands has proved deceptive.

The further aspect of Leavis which emerges by comparison with
Nietzsche's style is that, however difficult it may be, it bypasses
specialism. Its difficulty is not one by which an intelligent lay
reader is significantly disadvantaged. The difficulty lies rather in
its existential challenge; the *ad hominem* difficulty of a human
relationship rather than a specialist terminology for a complex of
ideas; although of course it encompasses that too. Nietzsche effects
an existential critique which transcends and subsumes philosophical activity. For this purpose he retains a tangible relation to
the common tongue. As I have said, it is not my intention to
compare Leavis with Nietzsche as a stylist or to make him an
honorary philosopher *malgré lui*. But the more striking, and
generally recognised, case of Nietzsche helps focus the conflicting
pressures implicitly at work in Leavis's language. He had in his
own way an awareness of the deceptions and seductions of which
language is the index and the means; he was using an established
field of enquiry while making that mode of enquiry the object of

his critique; and it was vital to his purpose to draw on the resources of the common idiom.

Conclusion

Hence there is a double recognition to be gained from comparing Leavis's sense of language with its nearest philosophical models. We can understand the considered significance he accorded to the 'creative' and 'enactive' potentialities of language and why these remained elusive of a general, theoretical description. They only exist at a certain level of particularity and participation. Heidegger, we might say, sets an agenda which Leavis carries out. But, by the same token, we can see how Leavis's unphilosophical discourse has, as part of its critical logic, a philosophical edge. He is aware of principled issues and his refusal to take them up in a theoretical way is in itself a principled and deliberate one. The fundamental recognition here is that poets, precisely as poets, *think*. And great poets think so profoundly that we can read them many times without realising that is what they are doing.[23] He was aware, too, that criticism can suffer the same fate. It is for this reason that I have highlighted his capacity as a 'thinker' by suggesting some philosophical parallels. But to bring out what he himself meant by critical, as opposed to philosophical, thinking we should note that his view of language entails a continuity between the literary works he discussed and the language in which he did so. In fact, the best points of reference in discussing him are the great creative writers, such as Blake, Eliot and Lawrence upon whom his own attention was centred. For that is precisely what he sought to do: not to imitate them, but to derive the fundamental terms of his criticism from them. Since poetry is in many respects the paradigmatic instance of literature for Leavis, I will consider first an essay on poetry and then, by extension from its terms, go on to consider his reading of prose fiction.

5

Poetry and Sincerity:
Leavis on Yeats

Leavis's understanding of the relation of language and experience is most clearly exemplified in his reading of English poetry. I propose, therefore, to sketch the principal lines of his reassessment of the English poetic tradition and then look closely at a particular occasion, a late lecture on Yeats, to see his premisses and his rhetoric in use.

Leavis endorsed the new assessment of the history of English poetry which was effected in his view largely by the creative, as well as the critical, example of T. S. Eliot. Although he came increasingly to perceive serious limitations and divisions in Eliot, Leavis always affirmed Eliot's unique achievement in bringing about this revolution in taste and in articulating its significance. Poundians, in particular, would perhaps wish to place some of the credit elsewhere and there is no doubt of Pound's importance to Eliot personally and to the modernist movement at large. But Eliot's inwardness with the evolution of English poetry and the ways in which he formulated its significance to himself as a contemporary poet made him for Leavis the crucial example. Leavis's critical preoccupations were very much of this generation and Eliot's essays in *The sacred wood* (1920) he acknowledged as among his first and most formative encounters with serious contemporary thinking about literature.

Now many of Eliot's early essays were written in journalistic circumstances in which he had little time to work out his intuitions or indeed the space to develop them if he had done. They tend, therefore, to have a pregnant but elusive suggestiveness about them. However, this quality may not be attributable purely to the circumstances of Eliot's early life in London. This exploratory way of

thinking, which combined sharply perceived qualities and rela-
tionships in texts with wide-ranging speculative reflections on their
significance, makes his criticism closely continuous with his
'creative' work as normally understood. Apart from the specific
insights and issues in Eliot's criticism, Leavis also picked up, I
would say, this sense of criticism as a form of creative discovery
through literature. Since Eliot was pre-eminently a poet, this
aspect of criticism gradually became less important to him. His
creative evolution is in his poetry. But Leavis developed a style of
criticism which, if less strikingly than in some of Eliot's essays, had
a fundamentally similar stance. Literature, both consciously and
unconsciously, was a form of discovery in the realms particularly
of feeling and response. The task of criticism is to articulate that
achievement as Eliot's essays had managed to do. It follows that if
poetry, in Eliot's later formulation, is 'a raid on the inarticulate',[1]
then criticism will have its own problems of an appropriate
articulacy. The danger for criticism will be of reducing the poet's
new or individual expression into the generality of the already
known. Leavis thought closely about an appropriate discourse for
dealing with major creative work; a discourse that would articulate
without reduction and judge without externalising. Hence in outlining how Leavis pursued Eliot's suggestive reading of English
poetry, I wish to emphasise particularly the act of reading as
rendered in his critical language.

In his early essays Eliot argued that romantic and Victorian
verse suffered from the increasing cultivation of an especially
'poetic' or dream world of feeling. Poetry so conceived tended to
be escapist in its very medium even when not overtly so at a
thematic level. In his search for contrary models of poetic expression in which all areas of experience could be handled seriously
and equally, he went back particularly to the period from Donne to
Marvell. In his essay on 'The metaphysical poets'[2] he identified
Dryden and Milton as the two powerful influences in which we can
see the subsequent 'dissociation of sensibility'.

It was this conception of English poetry as the index of a profound and damaging change in sensibility which became central to
Leavis's own account and underwrites its urgency. But in Leavis's
view Milton was a more troublesome figure than Dryden.
Dryden's virtues of rational and formal clarity were of a kind that
could be more readily externalised in reading and were correspondingly less subliminal in their influence. Hence he modified,
but did not so radically break, what Leavis called the 'line of wit'.

Like Eliot, Leavis emphasised the 'wit' that characterised several different schools of seventeenth-century verse; a quality not merely verbal and local but the manifestation of a poised and holistic grasp of experience. He traced the 'line of wit' down into the eighteenth century and was able thereby to focus the experiential complexity of Pope as the true basis of his greatness. Indeed, Leavis's account is partly responsible for the present high estimate of Pope; particularly as compared with Dryden. This reading, in short, posits a more powerful and intrinsic current than the external development of the Augustan couplet through Dryden, Denham and Waller.

The influence of Milton, in so far as it was damaging, was a more subtle and, as it turned out, a more controversial matter. Hence the greater attention given to it by Leavis. In his view the sonority of Milton's blank verse exerted an almost hypnotic power over later poets including major ones; a power which was most fatally manifest whenever they fell short of their own best inspiration. The Miltonic manner pulled away from the genius of the spoken English tongue and thereby helped to consolidate linguistically the special realm of the 'poetic'. The justice of this view of Milton will be considered later but it should be noted at this point that Leavis's case has what we might call a diagnostic, as well as an immediately critical, level to it. He was not in any simple way dismissive of Milton's achievement and he devoted a *Scrutiny* essay to defending Milton against his admirers.[3] But Leavis's sense of the creative and seductive potentialities of language, of how the quality of language governs the quality of experience individually and communally; led him to focus on the underlying nature and effects of Milton's style. He was not denying its power but pointing out what he saw as its corresponding danger. Such a language could not, in his view, explore and test experience in the creative and enactive manner.

Now in retrospect Eliot's broad analysis of both Victorian and seventeenth-century poetry may be seen as a creatively useful projection on his part while he was discovering and affirming his own poetic values. Poets often perceive literary history in the light of their own needs. As a matter of fact, Eliot came to revise, indeed effectively to reverse, his view of Donne and to dissociate himself from the phrase 'dissociation of sensibility'.[4] The two best accounts of the history and difficulties of this phrase are F. W. Bateson's essay entitled 'Dissociation of sensibility'[5] and the eighth chapter of Frank Kermode's *The romantic image*. Leavis,

59

however, always believed that there was something important at stake in the original perception that led Eliot to take up this formulation. He returned to the theme in the Clark lectures and defined it in a way that is explicitly indicative of his critical discourse at large. He opens the third lecture as follows:

> I know, of course, that 'sensibility' is a tricky word, one difficult to define for our purpose. But it is not for that any less an essential word. It can't, I think, be so fixed by definition as not to shift in force as we use it — as we find ourselves having to use it. But that is a peculiarity of important words — words we find we can't do without — in the field of our distinctive discipline of intelligence (for, I repeat, we ought to think of the distinctive discipline of literary study as that, and be able to justify the attitude). What the critic has to do is to cultivate a vigilant responsibility, so that the shifts confuse or mislead neither the reader nor himself. And 'sensibility' is a word to which the student ought to give a great deal of thoughtful attention; new perceptions and realisations are likely to result. There can hardly be a better text for bringing that home to him and starting fruitful discussion than this central, this pre-eminently focal criticism of Eliot's.

and after a brief comment on the twentieth-century relevance of the phrase he continues:

> The significance of this development, the history behind it and the consequences in twentieth-century literature, challenge the literary student to an enquiry of key importance for an intelligent grasp of English literary history. The criticism of Eliot's I am examining, and of which the scholars and academic critics in general have made so little, offers, in its pregnancy, (a matter of the significant concentration that goes with the 'axe to grind' and focuses an immense fund of force and suggestion), an incomparable opening into such an enquiry.[6]

These passages indicate very clearly the nature of critical discourse as Leavis understands it. The 'dissociation of sensibility' is not in itself an historical fact but rather a 'pregnant suggestion' and an 'opening' point for 'enquiry'. On the one hand there is the complex history of changed thought, feeling and ideas of personal

60

identity between 1600 and 1700 and on the other hand this epigrammatic formula. Leavis sees the phrase as a speculative and exploratory means rather than as a terminus. The obvious problem with this is that where the agenda of the enquiry is so set, the results are only too likely to confirm the suggested analysis. At the same time much would depend on the integrity of the enquiry. It would not have to be merely self-confirming. And that raises a further aspect of Leavis's use of the phrase.

He refers in this passage to Eliot's having an 'axe to grind' in his initial reading of seventeenth-century poetry. Far from disapproving of this, Leavis sees Eliot's critical intent as the basis of his historical insight. And in the same way Leavis's own reading of English poetry is animated by a critical purpose and in the light of a particular conception of personal and communal wholeness as embodied in language. The difficulty of the phrase, which Leavis recognises, lies in its denoting in the first instance a critical perception of the literary texts themselves; only inferentially, and as a consequence of that critical assessment, does it have an implication for historical understanding. The primacy of the critical question *vis-à-vis* historical considerations places Leavis's whole discourse in a highly problematic mode.[7] In effect, Leavis says of Eliot's phrase that there is an important recognition of quality at stake in it and no one has thought of a better, synoptic way of referring to it. And this is the explicit understanding of his own critical language at all times: it is shifting, assertive and fraught with speculative imponderables yet it is, he maintained, the means of effecting recognitions which apparently cannot be achieved in any other way.

Hence Leavis is always clear that the judgement of poetry is a judgement of the quality of life it embodies. Some readers will see this as too large and simple an assertion; others perhaps will see it as merely truistic. Either way it is unhelpfully vacuous as a generalisation. The effort of Leavis's critical practice is to generate a specific authority for such judgements and give a corresponding substance to the values invoked. To see how, and how effectively, he does this I propose to consider in some detail his late lecture entitled 'Yeats: the problem and the challenge'.[8] Returning in the mid-sixties to the topic of Yeats, on whom he had not significantly published since before the poet's death, the lecture is explicitly an attempt to reach a balanced *compte rendu* of the complete *œuvre*. In this later piece he is particularly self-conscious about the difficulty of defining and enforcing his judgements and it therefore helps us to focus the strengths and limitation of his critical posture.

Leavis opens by denying the self-proclaimed affinity of Yeats with Blake; an affinity largely accepted by critics. He contests this claim by noting the 'sincerity' of Blake as opposed to the pervasive striking of attitudes in Yeats. He pursues this case by a detailed appeal to 'Sailing to Byzantium' and 'Byzantium' followed by a brief comparison with 'Among school children'. He argues that, contrary to the conventional critical wisdom which sees 'Byzantium' as a deeper and more complex treatment of the 'Byzantium' theme, the later poem actually constitutes a narrowing and hardening of attitude. In this view, Yeats remains, of course, a great poet as in 'Among school children' but the relative displacing, if not to say 'dislodging', of 'Byzantium' is part of a larger claim that there are only a handful of poems which, on closer inspection, are of this quality. In particular, the relative simplicity of attitude seen in 'Byzantium' anticipates the rhetorical poses struck pervasively in Yeats's later verse such as 'Under Ben Bulben'. Ultimately, in Leavis's view, Eliot is the great poet of his generation, not Yeats.[9] I believe he is fundamentally right about Yeats but is unfair to 'Byzantium'. More importantly, his resistance to this poem is not arbitrary but characteristic in a way that defines a fundamental limit of his critical vision. Limitations, however, are often easier to define than the positive achievement without which they have no meaning. If we wish to identify the peculiarly Leavisian strength of the essay we must first consider very closely the term which Leavis himself emphasises as crucial: 'sincerity'.

Sincerity and impersonality

Ian Robinson has referred to Leavis's use of the word 'sincerity' as one of his original contributions to thought.[10] That suggests the significant gap between its everyday use and the special implication developed by Leavis. I have argued that the synoptic quality of Leavis's thinking in respect of language makes it necessary to amplify his central terms such as 'creative' and 'enactment' by their nearest philosphical analogies. So also some of Leavis's ethical terminology needs to be seen in a wider context for its particular intended force to be appreciated. Indeed, some readers who have attended apparently very closely to Leavis's terms have understood them with an almost parodic reductiveness because they have treated them without regard for their specifically evolved significances. 'Sincerity' is a case in point and there are two closely related aspects to be emphasised here. First, although the focus shifts with this word from the 'philosophical' to the 'ethical', its meaning for Leavis arises from the more general concern with language outlined in the preceding chapter. And second the implications of this term are properly to be understood only in their immediate historical context. For his use of the term 'sincerity' was the deliberate modification of a term widely used in Victorian criticism and largely discredited by the modernist generation. Rather than abandon the term, an issue to which I will return, Leavis redefined it in a way that constituted a challenging critique of modernism from within the terms of the modernist movement itself. In adducing Blake as the significant comparison with Yeats, Leavis was bringing his more general understanding of language to bear on the deceptively similar preoccupations of several modern writers. To see the force of this it is necessary to summarise some of the immediate provenance of the term 'sincerity' as inherited by these early twentieth-century authors.

A classic Victorian use of 'sincerity' as a literary criterion occurs in G. H. Lewes's *The principles of success in literature* (1869) in which he enumerates his three cardinal principles of 'clarity', 'sincerity' and 'beauty'. Lewes's book was conceived as a guide for aspirant writers rather than as literary theory and the first two of these principles in particular bear upon the creative process rather than the product. But Lewes is not concerned to draw this distinction for the effect of sincerity in the work is assumed to arise from the personal sincerity of the author. This is typical of Victorian usage in which the values of literature are frankly, although not necessarily naïvely, taken to be those of the author's personality.

By contrast, of course, it was one of the primary recognitions shared by diverse modern writers that the relation between the author and the work was, in this respect, at best problematic and often misleading. The author's personal sincerity is a dubious basis for literary quality; the verse on gravestones being an extreme instance of this truth. By the same token, the effect of sincerity in a literary text cannot in principle be used to infer the personal sincerity of the writer nor is the value of the work contingent upon doing so. Indeed, much of the programmatic thrust of modernism, albeit in very different ways, was to recognise the 'impersonal' aspect both of the creative act and of the work of literature. We might instance Joyce and Pound with their

Flaubertian emphasis on technique; D. H. Lawrence's dissatisfaction with the 'old stable ego' and his consequent search for new modes of narrative; T. S. Eliot's notion of the poet's creative 'escape from emotion', and, of course, Yeats's theory of the 'masks' referred to in Leavis's lecture. These are all manifestations of a suspicion of the apparently 'sincere' or 'personal' emotion in life and art. Since the essence of artistic creation is its transcendence of personal feeling, its value cannot be accounted for by primary reference to the author's personality.

But while the modern generation of writers may to this extent present a common front *vis-à-vis* their Victorian predecessors, they actually constitute a spectrum of different conceptions in which the extremes are mutually opposed. Leavis's insistence on 'sincerity' is not in opposition to modernist conceptions of impersonality but is rather a sharpening of their overall diagnostic value. His understanding of language gave him a more profound grasp of what 'impersonality' meant. He therefore resolved these partial and sometimes contradictory insights into a whole and coherent understanding essentially building, as he came to see, on the example of D. H. Lawrence. In retrospect it is possible to give a summary account of the perception that Leavis himself achieved by a gradually increasing recognition over several decades. To appreciate the force of this recognition consider first the two powerful and opposed conceptions of 'impersonality' represented respectively by Joyce and Lawrence.

Stephen Dedalus's aesthetic theory expounded in the last section of *A portrait of the artist as a young man*, however limited and jejune in its formulation by the character, is an essential Joycean manifesto and fairly indicates his Flaubertian allegiance. Joyce sought to remove the creator from the work by ever more diverse and elaborate means in *Ulysses*; means which may be largely subsumed under the heading of technique. Like Ezra Pound he emphasised the importance of technique in producing, and in his case foregrounding, the quality of impersonality. Lawrence, of course, is at the other extreme; his affinities in this respect are with Dickens and Dostoevsky. These writers are frankly personal to the point of being prophetic. Yet the prophet's voice, like the novelist's, is necessarily in some sense impersonal. The difference is that for them the impersonal is a quality of their explicit involvement in the subject and is, therefore, a quality achieved *within* and through the personality. Impersonality, in this conception, is not the minimum but the maximum degree of personality.[11] The image, in other words, is not of a creator removed and 'paring his fingernails' but of a creator so totally given to the work as to be transformed into its dramatic medium. A creator, indeed, more like the traditional Christian, rather than an atheist's, god.

Now shrewd readers have long recognised that this absolute opposition between the Joycean and the Lawrencean modes is in some respects more apparent than real. There comes a point at which the specific metaphors drop away; the fundamental necessity for authorial impersonality, considered as a general truth, is more essential than the vehicles it, perhaps arbitrarily, employs. But Leavis was not concerned with such general truths so much as with the differences in creative outlook between Joyce and Lawrence which are indeed reflected in these rival formulations. He saw that the rival ways of conceiving 'impersonality' were fraught with potential mystification and have for that reason a highly symptomatic value. That becomes particularly evident in respect of another influential figure in this domain: T. S. Eliot.

I have remarked that the impersonality sought by Joyce and Lawrence can, if stated abstractly, allow for a point on the circle where the extremes meet. And another reason why we might see the two imaginative universes producing a cognate recognition is that each conception of impersonality is coherent, comprehensive and enabling within its own world. Each of them knew very well, artistically, what he was doing. However, when we pass to Eliot, as Leavis was principally responsible for showing, there is a revealing disjuncture between the critical principle and its rhetorical formulation. Eliot's essay 'Tradition and the individual talent' contains in its first part some of his most illuminating and deservedly influential discussion of the meaning of tradition followed in the second part by some of his most tendentious theorising about the artistic process.[12] A key element in Leavis's evolving assessment of the modernist generation is his gradual shift from endorsement of the former to a diagnostic understanding of the latter.[13] The second section of Eliot's essay ends with this now notorious formula:

> Poetry is not a turning loose of emotion, but an escape from emotion; it is not the expression of personality, but an escape from personality. But, of course, only those who have personality and emotions know what it means to want to escape from these things. (*Selected essays*, p. 21)

65

Now that we know more about Eliot's personal life at the time we can appreciate the plangency of his arch attempt to bully the reader in this final sentence. But the unhappy relation to feeling registered in this remark only reinforces the more crucial oddity of the word 'escape' in the preceding sentence. Eliot is making a proper and, in its time, very important discrimination between the merely personal and the artistically significant domains of feeling. This could have been expressed by some more neutral term such as 'objectify' or 'transcend' but the word 'escape' implies both a negative view of the personal feeling and an actual departure from it. Now, once again, the fundamental recognition at issue here is elusive of precise formulation — if an emotion is artistically transmuted is it still that emotion? But our concern is precisely with the attitudes enshrined in the metaphors. What emerges very clearly in Eliot's account is that poetic emotion is being imaged as an alternative to personal feeling rather than as a fuller possession of it. The symptomatic nature of his metaphor here suggests a broader interpretation of the modernist preoccupation with impersonality.

The programmatic emphasis on impersonality in the modernist generation was properly corrective of the romantic aftermath whether in creative literature or in the common perception of it. Sentimentality, moral rhetoric and the cult of personality were all possible corruptions of clear thinking and true feeling. Joyce saw his own nation paralysed with false sentiment in religion and politics; Pound saw his generation sent to the trenches of the Great War in which, we might now say, the horror of poison gas was a fitting symbol of the noisome political atmosphere. There was everything at stake for these writers in insisting on a tough truthfulness of language. And Joyce's choice of Homer, an epic poet, and Shakespeare, a renaissance dramatist, as the tutelary presences behind the modern action of *Ulysses* suggests a more comprehensive historical analysis whereby the evolution of our culture has made an impersonal view of experience harder to achieve. Indeed, it is precisely an achievement rather than a given quality of being. But once we can distinguish between a quality of being and a conscious project we open a possible disjuncture between the purpose and the method. Hence the highly conscious method by which an author seeks to meet the criterion of impersonality may place that author in an increasingly loaded, preemptive relation to his own relevant emotional experience. The preoccupation with impersonality as an achievement *within* the work may distract the author, and reader, from inspection of the personal sources *from* which the work has been created. *The waste land* is now a widely recognised, classic instance of this principle. There is a disjuncture between the sexual fertility approved at the impersonal level of its central myth and the personal disgust in the presentation of its sexual episodes. Neither the techniques of impersonality, nor the conscious aesthetic commitment to it, can guarantee the achievement of it and may indeed constitute precisely the symptom of a fundamental anxiety, or failure, in that area. The celebration of impersonality can be a mystification; the technique an unwitting alibi. If this is relatively easy to see with hindsight that is partly owing to Leavis's detailed analyses of these authors along with crucial exemplary figures such as Blake. This was the recognition behind Leavis's increasingly radical critique of T. S. Eliot and his corresponding commitment to D. H. Lawrence. He came to see Lawrence's very vulnerability, even his manifest errors, as part of an exemplary self-exploration that achieved its representative, or impersonal, value through its open-handedness and its directness of purpose. Impersonal understanding of the emotional domain is achieved in the risky arena of the self.

In the brief concluding section of his essay Eliot distinguishes 'sincere' emotion in 'verse' from 'significant' emotion in 'poetry':

> There are many people who appreciate the expression of sincere emotion in verse, and there is a smaller number of people who can appreciate technical excellence. But very few know when there is an expression of *significant* emotion, emotion which has its life in the poem and not in the history of the poet. (*Selected essays*, p. 22)

This provides the cue for Leavis's use of the word 'sincerity'. Leavis saw a pervasive habit of equivocation in Eliot when Eliot was not 'thinking' as a poet. The present passage is an example of the kind of thing he had in mind. Logically, Eliot is merely distinguishing between 'sincerity' and 'significance' but rhetorically he is implying that they are mutually opposed. Hence the relation between them is blurred and it is to the clarification of this representative confusion that Leavis's use of 'sincerity' is addressed.

In the course of the Yeats lecture Leavis finds it necessary on several occasions to define 'sincerity':

> Poetic success here means a kind of convincingness and inevitability that comes of, that *is*, complete sincerity — the sincerity that is of the whole being, not merely a matter of conscious intention. (p. 65)

> It has the livingness of enacted self-discovery, brought by the technical skill of the poet to the satisfyingness of a complete poem — analogically a musical satisfyingness, and for us an index of sincerity. (p. 72)

and perhaps most notably:

> I don't myself believe that Blake had any comprehensive guiding wisdom to offer, but it was his genius to be capable of a complete disinterestedness, and therefore of a complete sincerity. He had a rare integrity, and a rare sense of responsibility as a focus of life. His experience was *his* because only in the individual focus can there *be* experience, but his concern to perceive and understand was undeflected by egotism, or by any impulse to protect an image of himself. (p. 77)

The peculiarly parenthetical, sidelong introduction of the central term here is an aspect of the definition. He is holding together both G. H. Lewes's use of 'sincerity' and the modern emphasis on 'impersonality'; or at least what is really essential to each of them. The important difference from Lewes is that Leavis's definition is entirely inductive. It appeals to the demonstrable features of the text and seeks no biographical support. But at the same time it preserves the holism of Lewes's usage. The achievement of the poem, in so far as it represents a command of experience, is the achievement of the poet and this remains the case even if this command only ever occurs within the writing of the poem. The poem is an index of moral sensibility which may well not be coterminous with the historical Blake or Yeats. Indeed, it is a large part of Leavis's case in this lecture that Yeats's best poetry is precisely not representative of the man. But the sensibility in the poem is none the less the poet's and the success of the poem cannot be affirmed without a judgement, albeit an implicit one, of the life values it involves. In the same way, 'technical skill' is a means for the poet and an index for the reader but it never becomes an explanation of the poem's success or failure. Hence also, perhaps, Leavis's unproblematic reference to the speaking voice of the poetry as

'Yeats' or 'Blake'. Even when he is not thinking at the synoptic level of this lecture, an explicit distinction between the poem's 'speaker' and the historical poet is usually felt by Leavis to be otiose and potentially debilitating. He observes the essential spirit of this modern critical distinction by his scrupulous adherence to the text as the inferential medium through which the poet is known, but within these terms of reference he wishes to define the achievement *of* the poem, we might say, rather than the achievement *within* it. While a poem's speaker can be seen almost as a separable dramatic character, Leavis seeks to identify the 'enacted self-discovery' which this voice, or the use of this voice, represents.

Hence in Leavis's use of the term 'sincerity' both elements are vital: the 'biographical' and the 'purely textual'. For Leavis, 'sincerity' is not the counter-term to 'impersonality' but its necessary basis and the value of this dual emphasis lies in the more searching and three-dimensional focus on impersonality that it entails. The last of the above quotations enforces the meaning of sincerity as disinterestedness and the formulation there is particularly sharp in that Leavis is explicitly sceptical of Blake's 'wisdom' at any level of content or didactic intent. In so far as his poetry has a moral significance, this lies in its very presentation of experience. It is not to be found in some prior value inherent in the experience as 'life' nor in some principled truth statable independently of the work itself.

Impersonality and the critic

We might say then that Leavis's use of 'sincerity' infused a Victorian moral category with a modernist understanding to produce a critical criterion more testable than the former and more testing than the latter. It transcends the 'biographical' and the 'technical' fallacies by properly understanding, and relating, their respective truth values. In this regard it reflects his dual commitment to the English critical tradition and to the 'new bearings' made possible by the modern movement. But it is most essentially enabled by his meditation on the nature of language. By the same token the deliberately central use of this notoriously difficult term epitomises the characteristic stance of his critical language which has to be understood in the first instance at what we might call a dispositional rather than a principled level. His language represents a fundamental posture which it is necessary to identify first because it is the basis of any more separably definable procedures in his practice.

I have devoted considerable space to the exposition of a term which, even on the evidence of Leavis's own lecture, seems very susceptible of misunderstanding. Leavis's prose when introducing the term has a strained, parenthetical movement combined with an asseverative pressure. Yet, even so, readers have been known to take his term simply in its everyday moral sense. Would it not have been easier, one might ask, to develop some other locution for this specialised meaning? We should pause on what is at stake for Leavis here since it relates to his fundamental conviction that great writers like Shakespeare and Dickens are in an important sense the *products* of the common language. I have already remarked on Leavis's resistance to the scientism that often accompanies a specialised terminology. Against the growth of a professional, technical discourse for the discussion of literature, Leavis maintained the importance of common usage. Yet there is more involved here than resistance to scientism: it is an attempt to establish a particular kind of authority.

Critical vision is characteristically bi-focal in that behind the complex and sophisticated discriminations of viewpoint and irony, etc. which constitute literary reading there is an apodictic recognition of values for which, in Leavis's view, the nearest approach to an authoritative standard of reference is the usage of the speech community in question. I say the 'nearest approach' since the terms of common usage are in themselves neither fixed nor authoritative and they are themselves therefore to be tested and sharpened in their turn against moments of consummate expression such as great poems provide. Something like this mutual definition is happening with the word 'sincerity'. That is why even in such a late piece he finds it appropriate several times over to define the term afresh. It may well be that had he just used the word without this special emphasis experienced readers would have recognised its significance. Yet that might in itself mean that it had ossified into a term of art and lost its moral charge. Or we can imagine him perhaps using the term 'authenticity' which, as Lionel Trilling has pointed out, implies much of the modernist emphasis on an intrinsic standard that Leavis was seeking to infuse into the word 'sincerity'.[14] But 'authenticity' precisely does not carry that charge of intimately personal and social responsibility for which the term 'sincerity' is irreplaceable. Leavis is using this word not only because he has to, but because he wants to. His intent is to recharge and refine upon the meaning of a word indispensable not just in literary criticism but in the common tongue. His usage has in itself a creative purpose. Typically he is as intent here on defining 'sincerity' as he is on his account of Blake or Yeats. The word is emphasised to enforce the identity of the 'literary' and the 'extra-literary' domains which the exigencies of analysis encourage us to dualise. The characteristic strenuousness of Leavis's language arises from the way it creates and questions its terms while seeking to hold the two domains in a single vision. The impact of Leavis's best criticism lies in the penetration and accuracy with which he defines moral or emotional quality in the work. There is no reason, perhaps, why such criticism should ultimately be any more explicable than a poem. But in so far as we can identify its bases rhetorically, it crucially involves his ability to use the resources of the common tongue. He reflected constantly on the paradox, if it is one, that the distinctive voice of a great poet was also the most representative use of the contemporary language. That, indeed, is precisely the issue at stake for him in this lecture as between Blake and Yeats. And he locates this quality most essentially, as we have seen, in a disposition *towards* the language rather than in what is actually *said*.

The general critical problem that Leavis's criticism especially foregrounds is that of authority. How are the critic's judgements anything more than, in the weak sense, a matter of 'taste' or 'opinion'? The issue is peculiarly salient in Leavis's case because of his radical cultural critique and his frontal engagement with the issues it raises. What has been said so far indicates something of the criterion that Leavis himself brings to this issue. For the value of impersonality cannot be divisible and it is in some respects an even more self-evident requirement for a critic than it is for a poet. And in criticism, as in poetry, the nettle of personality has to be grasped: a technically produced discourse of impersonality may be as illusory in the one sphere as in the other. Hence, Leavis's comments on Blake provide the standard for his own criticism as well as for later poets. Blake's 'rare integrity' and his 'sense of responsibility as a focus of life' are the implicit criteria for the critic. They are not the less essential or demanding for being moral rather than 'theoretical' premisses of critical practice. Despite the elusiveness of such qualities, it is worth probing analytically the rhetorical forms in which they are manifest. For Leavis's attempts to draw creatively and critically from the most common resources of the language will involve, where successful, something of the impersonally representative, or dramatic, use of the personal voice that he recognised on a different scale in great poets. There is no lack of 'personality' in Leavis's criticism. But how well, we may ask, does he fare by the standard he is invoking for Blake and Yeats?

There are several dimensions to this. One is that Leavis's practice constantly emphasises personality as the indispensable means which must at the same time be transcended. The opening page of the Yeats lecture is characteristic. He starts with a bold, synoptic statement: 'Yeats, for all his conviction of an essential affinity, was radically unlike Blake.' But this is precisely an assertion not an argument and he goes on in the rest of the paragraph to indicate that this will not be the explicit thread of the ensuing discussion. The second paragraph then makes a series of backward or lateral steps indicating the difficulty, and particularly the difficulty for him, of getting started on his theme. He says, for example, 'I am committed, I had been inclined to say, to some rashness; but "rashness" suggests irresponsibility, so I withdraw the word.' This sentence enacts a doubleness for which Jacques Derrida has provided a useful term: 'erasure'. Leavis has clearly not withdrawn the word from the reader's field of consciousness yet he simultaneously signals its unsuitability for his purpose. It is quite appropriate that Derrida who has attacked most radically the 'metaphysics of presence' in philosophical and critical prose, and who therefore occupies the diametrically opposed position to Leavis's 'frank' highlighting of personality, should provide the nearest conceptual term for what Leavis is doing. Not only do the extremes meet but Leavis's prose is highly aware of the problem of presence in accommodating it to the purposes of criticism. The combination of syntactical strain and resilient sense in his prose is the equivalent of what for another writer might constitute a separably theoretical domain. It is helpful, if a little paradoxical, to see the whole emphatic dimension of personality in Leavis's prose as 'under erasure'.

For Leavis's prose style consists largely in the avoidance of 'style'. It is difficult for a forceful and individual voice not to become a self-image and the protection of a self-image is what Leavis identified in his remarks on Blake as the principal threat to disinterestedness. Of course, this does not mean that he literally has no characteristic manner any more than it does with respect to Blake. He can be characteristic to the point of self-parody. I am speaking rather of a significant rhetorical effect which is part of his meaning. While he cannot literally avoid having a recognisable personal style, he enacts a constant refusal to allow a stylistic momentum, an obstructive or separable self-projection, to develop. In so far as he can meet this problem literally he does so by foregrounding it. In fact, like Dr Johnson he has moments of deliberate self-parody. His style is designed not for the delivery of judgements but for consciously enacting the difficulty of arriving at them. The authority of the judgement lies in the specific act of attention it recreates dramatically for the reader. It is indicative in this regard that the Yeats lecture *is* a lecture originally delivered to an audience and preserves in its published form references which apply only to that occasion as, for example, his regret that there is not time for a complete reading of 'Sailing to Byzantium'. There are no doubt extrinsic and practical reasons for this but it is intrinsically appropriate. Dramatically, his criticism always recreates itself as an occasion of recognition and his style reflects the Platonic distrust of written language as an ossification of thought. In so far as this entails a commitment to the 'metaphysics of presence', the presence is modelled upon a Blakean 'identity' rather than 'self-hood'. This is a demanding standard and what is remarkable is not that he ever fails to meet it, but that he so often succeeds. His style enacts the attempt as its way of affirming the implicit criterion.

Leavis's style, it should be apparent, is an awareness of complex possibilities both to assimilate and to avoid. The immediately preceding remarks have emphasised one aspect of this: his avoidance of an obtrusive or obfuscatory self-image; the immanent presence of the self as 'stylist'. But recognising the personal existential commitment on which the critical function rests, and the impossibility of the author's literal self-effacement, we have to consider how his rhetoric also poses personality as, not just a necessary, but a positive term. It is, after all, the damaging effect of self-image that is in question, not personality itself. Far from it. Leavis is the paradigm case for the truth that critical authority is personal authority. And if the idea of 'erasure' seems indeed too negative and oblique a way of putting the point, the critic's instrumental use of his personal voice can also be put in more positive and familiar terms. For this purpose we may turn to another great poet on whom Leavis has also written in ways that reflect interestingly upon himself.

I have already remarked that Leavis had a part in the modern rehabilitation of Pope. Underlying the recognition of Pope's poetic vitality is an appreciative acceptance of Pope's satiric stance as legitimate and necessary. The common Victorian view of Pope as a kind of malicious dwarf reduced satire to temperament. Modern readings of Pope are likely to emphasise, by contrast, how the personal dimension in Pope is used and transformed for a legitimate satiric purpose. Thus Maynard Mack has countered the temperamental reduction of Pope by noting the irreducibly personal basis of his satire and then demonstrating how Pope uses the conventions of the satiric tradition to transpose his personal self into what is essentially a satiric persona. For Pope, he says, the muse of satire 'is a not entirely playful symbol of the satiric genre — its rhetorical and dramatic character'.[15] The force of Mack's point lies in the delicacy of the gradations he indicates between 'poet' and 'persona'. Much of the weight of the satire lies in the poet's speaking with the pressure of personal experience in real historical circumstances yet this '*propria persona*' voice must also be understood as a dramatic, or at least as a dramatically controlled, one. Hence to call it a 'persona' as opposed to the voice of the poet is seriously to reduce the poem while thinking of it as simply personal is equally reductive. Mack identifies this minimal but crucial aspect of self-dramatisation in Pope as the proper point on the spectrum for his satire. Matters of moral or social permissibility are negotiated as rhetorical understandings.

Leavis's criticism involves him in the same fundamental assertion of what Mack, invoking the satiric conventions, calls '*laus et vituperatio*; praise and blame'. This is not to suggest that the voice of Leavis's criticism should be seen as a 'persona'; that would run counter to its whole thrust. But there is a crucial dramatic consciousness in his self-presentation. The enactive, moment-by-moment thinking process of the prose is also a way of dramatising, and thereby instrumentalising, the self. The deliberate strenuousness of the expression is closely allied to his wit as it is in Henry James. It is not ornamental wit separable from statement. Leavis was a formidable controversialist because his ironic command was not of the extrinsic debating kind but completely intrinsic to his grasp of the subject.

From this point of view the opening page of the Yeats lecture serves in large part to establish the speaker. His prose enacts its constant agon of self-awareness as the implicit basis for disinterested vision. This running presentation of his interior drama of response as a representative instrument of critical vision has struck some readers as a monstrous or tiresome, because irrelevant, imposition of personality while for others it constitutes a clear and open-handed source of authority. The test case, perhaps, is his Richmond lecture on the then C. P. Snow's 'The two cultures'. This is the piece in which Leavis approaches most overtly the satiric mode. It is destructive, personal, and done with evident relish. He was widely condemned, although also supported, for this and Snow was evidently bewildered as to what 'personal' motives could have led to the unprovoked 'attack' on him. The lecture seems to me to be justified on the Popean model both in its essential point and, having accepted that, in its manner. His opening play on the 'portentous' nature of Snow has Popean affinities and is not ornamental to the case being made.[16] In the nature of the case it could not have been done moderately or without personalities. Its essential burden is not philosophical, but situational. Yet for the purpose it has been done disinterestedly. Whether you find it acceptable or not, it is the sharpest example of what the ideal of disinterestedness might entail. 'Personality', far from being its opposite, may be its necessary vehicle. If Leavis's posture in this striking, but not unrepresentative, instance resembles a classically satiric one it is worth noting his own comment a few years later, *à propos* some lines of T. S. Eliot, that they are the nearest approach that could be made in our time to great satire.[17] Leavis's criticism requires some of the same conditions of consensus that satire does.

All this is to indicate what Leavis means by disinterestedness and how that relates to the critic's authority. Clearly, to invoke Blake's 'rare sense of responsibility as a focus of life' is to propose a standard that could hardly be expressed as a method although Leavis, like a poet, developed a 'voice' for it. Hence the circuitous shifts I have adopted to indicate the implication of the Leavisian posture; his attempts to square the circle of being at once there and not there in the act of reading. That Leavis's criticism needs to be approached critically rather than just philosophically is evidenced by the way in which philosophical analyses seem repeatedly to be accurate and yet beside the point as accounts of his actual critical impact. Hence my preference for literary artists as the appropriate points of reference. This is not, of course, to put him on a footing with them but to indicate the mode of attention he gives and therefore requires of his reader, not, as it were, for himself but on behalf of the author. In this lecture on Yeats he invokes, through Blake, a serious criterion which, if it is taken seriously at all, must be seen as a profound one. Then with a minimum of interpretation or gloss, indeed with a straight reading of the poem as its ideal centre, he re-presents the Yeats poems in the light of a felt scale of values. This ability to invoke a pertinent, vital and impersonal scale of values from the most common resources of the language is the basis of what he means by 'grounded judgement' and it is well exemplified in his reading of Yeats.[18]

The Byzantium poems

Leavis's authority, then, lies in a clear and disinterested understanding of 'centrally human' values and in putting these existential cards clearly on the table. It is an Antaeus principle of keeping one foot firmly on a common scale of significances. The frame of reference is never trivial and it is always in focus. But this does not mean that his judgements, for all their striving for disinterestedness, are necessarily just and indeed the existential holism that characterises his critique has a double-edged value for the present study. Leavis's assessment of 'Byzantium', which he offers as an epitomising one in respect of Yeats's *œuvre*, is as much a reflection on him as on Yeats. It is, therefore, worth looking closely at his reading of this poem which has, I believe, an epitomising value with respect to Leavis himself.

Leavis begins by noting the general assessment of 'Byzantium' as a richer, more complex achievement than 'Sailing to Byzantium'. In going on to contest this view he attributes it to the predilection of Yeats scholars for poems requiring the specialist knowledge of Yeatsian ideas to which they have devoted their careers. There may be some empirical truth in that but, as Leavis himself goes on to argue, the poem is not so crucially dependent on such knowledge and the suggestion is really a distraction arising, we might say, from a failure of disinterestedness on Leavis's part; a failure which may be symptomatic. For the critical issue is whether this poem indeed expresses merely a bitterness towards the conditions of life; a bitterness which, as Leavis claims, narrows and blunts the poet's responsiveness. In his view it allows for only one stratum of feeling as opposed to the openness and ambivalence of 'Sailing to Byzantium'.

What this reading importantly misses, I believe, is that the poem expresses a particular mood. As a mood it is, of course, totalising; it encompasses everything while it lasts. But however recurrent and important a particular mood may be it is not necessarily the whole and considered view of life espoused by the poet. The critical relevance of this lies in the way the mood is used by the poem as a *donnée*. The bitter yearning to escape the conditions of life is set in opposition to the ecstatic vision of a mystical alternative so that it is only half of a more complex totality. Leavis might reply that the vision is merely the product of a bitter rejection of life; a reiteration of it rather than an alternative. But the structure and carefully developed climax of the poem oblige us, at the very least, to see the bitterness as a dramatically controlled and consciously enabling premiss for the final vision. Once the initial polarity of a this-wordly bitterness and a transcendental yearning have been set up they are used in an increasingly interpenetrative and testing dialectic and therein lies the case for its being a more complex and intense work than 'Sailing to Byzantium'. It is not my intention to bandy personal readings with Leavis but I should summarise what I take to be the opposed, and more positive reading, of 'Byzantium' to bring out how Leavis's larger conception of poetry and language is reflected in his detailed response.

In 'Sailing to Byzantium' the urge to transcendence in art and eternity found as its ultimate embodiment a kind of clockwork toy and this note of anti-climax in turn focused retrospectively the undercurrent of nostalgia for lost youth which had accompanied the initial desire for art.

> Once out of nature I shall never take
> My bodily form from any natural thing,
> But such a form as Grecian goldsmiths make
> Of hammered gold and gold enamelling
> To keep a drowsy Emperor awake;
> Or set upon a golden bough to sing
> To lords and ladies of Byzantium
> Of what is past, or passing, or to come.

The poem is indeed finely balanced but at the expense of an impasse. In 'Byzantium', by contrast, Yeats tried to overcome this and the final vision is a supremely intense one of fire, music and dance enacted in the imagined present.

> Astraddle on the dolphin's mire and blood,
> Spirit after spirit. The smithies break the flood,
> The golden smithies of the Emperor.
> Marbles of the dancing floor

> Break bitter furies of complexity,
> Those images that yet
> Fresh images beget,
> That dolphin-torn, that gong-tormented sea.

It is a pre-eminently dynamic and passionate vision that seeks to transpose and intensify, rather than just escape, the emotional life. Its richer paradox is that the transcendent vision is itself passionately conceived. His imaginative identification now is not with the art objects but with the activity of creating them; an activity which itself is not an 'eternal now' so much as a continuing present guaranteed by the infinite fecundity of life. Moreover, the stanza shape expresses a releasing and containing of energy in the penultimate short lines followed by the final longer one in which the rhyme and the sense are brought to a closure. The stanza form is itself dynamic where that of 'Sailing to Byzantium' is monumental. The movement of the poem effects a dynamic balance as finely poised as the blend of passionate yearning and ontological scepticism from which the vision arises. In short, the poem is even more intensely affirmative, and proportionately self-questioning, than 'Sailing to Byzantium'.

As it happens the dialectical and self-questioning aspect of Yeats's poetry is further reinforced and subtilised by his construction of an overall *œuvre*. The mutual self-reference of individual poems both relativises and defines their particular moods. We understand them more sharply in appreciating their partiality. Hence the poignancy of 'Among school children', which Leavis rightly adduces as one of Yeats's supreme poems, is enhanced by its enacted recognition of the deeply misguided, or at least insidious, nature of the impulse underlying the Byzantium poems. Yet Yeats does not 'reject' these poems in the light of it nor do we expect him to in reading it. It is rather that the Byzantium impulse is 'bracketed' by the rest of the *œuvre* including 'Among school children'. This effect of the *œuvre* is not achieved just retroactively as an effect of putting all these disparate poems together; it draws on something they have in common: the controlled self-dramatisation of his moods, the 'bracketing' of his commitment, even within the individual poems.

Now Leavis sees the self-dramatisation clearly enough; that is the principal burden of his critique. But he does not accept the positive significance it achieves by framing the material of the poems in a special way. He does not accept Yeats's relativistic stepping back from his experience in this fashion. Whether he actually sees it and deliberately discounts it, or whether he just does not see it at all, is hard to say because he writes it so completely out of his account. I have already noted Leavis's tendency to elide the distinction between poet and speaker which is customarily insisted on in modern criticism. He is concerned with the handling of experience irrespective of its immediate dramatic or formal attribution, and where the speaker *per se* is not demonstrably subjected to critical perception as part of the poem's action then such narrative indirection is likely for him to represent an evasion or uncertainty in the poet. The poem is likely to have lost its grip. As I have repeatedly emphasised, the directness of his critique in this respect does not imply any literalistic conception of mimesis. Leavis fully recognises that poetry must be distinct from life if it is to offer a significant mimetic comment on, or model of, experience. What he does not, I think, accept is that poetry may produce such purely speculative states for the sake of which fundamental human values are to be held in abeyance. The *referential* bracketing, the 'suspension of disbelief', intrinsic to poetic meaning cannot, for him, be extended to an *evaluative* bracketing. Leavis's comments on 'Byzantium', and to that extent on much of the Yeatsian *œuvre*, rest on this underlying principle. But many of Yeats's poems express whole moral truths by recognising that they cannot express *the* whole truth. Yeats's perfectly conscious relativism, as built into the fundamental premises of his poetry, is part of his claim to a representative value as a major modern poet. His is not just one view within a pluralistic world: he has expressed a pluralistic consciousness within his own most personal affirmations. Hence Yeats's claim lies not necessarily in the expression of wholeness but in the clarity and integrity of his concern for it. As he said late in his life:

> I think that two conceptions, that of reality as a congeries of beings, that of reality as a single being, alternate in our emotion and in history and must always remain something that human reason, because subject always to one or the other, cannot reconcile. I am always, in all I do, driven to a moment which is the realisation of myself as unique and free, or to a moment which is the surrender to God of all that I am . . . Could these two impulses, one as much a part of the truth as the other, be reconciled, or if the one or other could prevail, all life would cease.[19]

This passage contains the rhetorical inflation, the being half in love with his condition, that Leavis identified in Yeats's poetry. But there is also a serious recognition that wholeness does not lie just within the will and that the struggle itself is creative for him. This is an aspect, perhaps the aspect, of modern culture that Leavis cannot accept: its pluralistic relativism. Where Yeats says that 'the centre cannot hold', Leavis replies that it *must* hold. Yeats's poetry attempts to achieve at least moments of wholeness within this relativistic frame of reference: for Leavis this is a self-contradiction. Leavis's intent focus on poetry as a holistic index of being cannot accommodate this degree of speculative obliquity in the framing of the poetic experience.

This point is cardinal to Leavis's criticism and it may be amplified by some comments of E. D. Hirsch on the notion of 'bracketing' in Husserl and Heidegger. Husserl, he says:

> posited the mind's capacity to 'bracket' a domain of experience so that the domain could be contemplated over time. 'Bracketing', then, is a simplified, visual metaphor for our ability to demarcate not only a content but also the mental acts by which we attend to that content, apart from the rest of our experience. This demarcation, corresponding to the distinction between meaning and significance, alone assures the potential sameness of objects in experience over time.

For Heidegger, Husserl's ideas pertaining to bracketing suggested an excessively abstract cognitive model that left out of account the fullness of the experienced life through which we know something in the world. So in place of brackets, Heidegger took as his model a more expansive epistemic form: the circle, the hermeneutic circle as expounded by Dilthey. The two forms or models are for Heidegger quite antithetical in their implications. The hermeneutic circle is based on the paradox that we must know the whole world in a general way *before* we know a part, since the nature of the part as such is determined by its function in the larger whole. Of course, since we can know a whole only through its parts, the process of interpretation is a circle. Experience as we interpret it must, by the compulsion of logic, follow this circular pattern. But since we must in some sense pre-know a whole before we know a part, every experience is pre-constituted by the whole context in which it is experienced. On this model, it is *impossible* to bracket off one part of experience and separate it from the whole of experienced life. What we know at any time is 'pre-conceptually' known and constituted by the whole of our world, and since that world changes in time, so must the objects (for us) change which that world pre-constitutes. The 'artificial' brackets have been swept away, and replaced with the fullness of lived experience.[20]

Hirsch goes on to argue that neither of these models can be given the full weight their proponents have claimed for them and Husserl's proposal seems to him the stronger in that it was always to be understood as a possible, rather than a necessary, mode of thought. And I have already noted that Heidegger also modified his position later. But Hirsch's summary brings out the resistance to bracketing that follows from the Heideggerian conception; a resistance which is comparable to Leavis's.

As a focus of mental attention the act of bracketing can be understood in a weaker and stronger sense. We may focus attention on an experience, without as it were interfering with it. Or on the other hand we may take an experience and remove it from its natural or historical matrix in order to subject it to some special pressure or distortion. The analogy would be scientific observation. We can simply observe processes in nature. But we can also subject natural elements to laboratory conditions in which their limits or interactions can be discovered in ways that natural circumstances would never allow. Comparably, a poet may express an experience within the matrix of the reader's assumed world. In such a case the artist, as Henry James was very aware, will have implicitly to define the necessary boundaries of the work without falsity with respect to this larger world. We expect the artist not to distort our world. But there is a different kind of poem in which the poet in effect asks: what would happen if I pushed this particular impulse, or mood, to an extreme that life would not permit? Here a different understanding has to be established whereby the implied relation to the world, if expressed mathematically, would require a negative symbol; or perhaps the separation sign of the bracket. As with a laboratory experiment, care has to be taken to allow for its conditional basis but insights and intensities can be produced within it for which there is no other arena. Of course, in the poetic context, these contractual understandings with the reader are usually implicit ones; making them explicit would often damage the delicacy of the experience like opening the door of a pressure chamber. And Yeats is particularly subtle in covering his tracks, partly because of his strategic, natural-seeming premiss of dramatised self-consciousness. He speaks in a homely way of 'mood' and 'dream' not of relativity and hypothesis. But in many of his poems, such as those mentioned here, he uses this self-communing as a conditioning framework. That is not, of course, to be taken in a biographical sense. Whether or not Yeats, as Pound said, actually believed in 'spooks', for example, is strictly neither here nor there. The point is that the poems, particularly as set in the *œuvre*, have this implicit contract built in. It is indicative that Leavis speaks of Yeats's poetic self-communings as 'reverie' rather than, say, 'dialogue', which *is* their characteristic structure and is an equally Yeatsian term. Leavis's word suggests a relaxation of attention rather than a heightening of it. When Yeats spoke of Bertrand Russell as 'feather-headed' he was reflecting on the complex and precise understandings that govern his own utterances even when they seem simple, sensuous and passionate.

I have approached the issue in this way through Yeats and the notion of 'bracketing' because he highlights what is really at stake for Leavis. It is not simply a matter of 'narrowness' of taste. But the more general way of expressing the application of this point in literary critical terms would be to say that Leavis resists any poetic contract with the reader depending upon a distinctive category of the 'aesthetic'. He often remarked, in dismissive asides, that the term 'aesthetic' is best avoided in criticism.[21] That is a shrewd point. In the long hangover from 1890s aestheticism and with the tendency to appeal to 'aesthetic' taste as a convenient justification of conventional, or merely social, judgements it is undoubtedly a term to scrutinise. But the whole complex category of the aesthetic is not therefore to be dismissed just by sturdy British common sense. As it happens the English tradition, for which Leavis is more a representative voice than an external commentator, throws up fewer, and less troublesome, cases of writers requiring the conscious evaluative bracketing for which the aesthetic category has to be evoked. Continental European tradition has figures such as Baudelaire whose greatness, Theodor Adorno has remarked, 'was so unequivocally tied up with the absence of *mens sana*'. But the absence of such striking cases may conceal rather than remove the problem. Even English poetry may require in some measure not just a 'willing suspension of disbelief' but a suspension of our fundamental existential commitments. The aesthetically bracketed relativism of Yeats allows us to identify the point of principle that defines, as a boundary, Leavis's area of strength. His conception of creativity in language actively excludes such an interpretation of the artistic domain. The aesthetic, taken in this stronger, speculative sense, is for Leavis an abnegation of the wholeness of being that underlies the greatest poetry. It is in itself a form of irresponsibility.

Within these terms, his strength emerges clearly in this Yeats lecture. It is not just in the questioning of the *œuvre* to see how much of it is actually of Yeats's own best achievement. It is in the tactical placing of Yeats next to Blake, and thus using an already intimate point of reference, so that the nature of the poetic voice is clearly identified. And, indeed, my own comments on what Leavis's reading misses are not intended to supplant, only to qualify, it. Undoubtedly, Yeats's projection of a self-image remains fundamental to his creativity and the extent to which he manages to turn this into a subject-matter or a controlling poetic means is properly open to diagnostic attention of the kind that Leavis gives. Hence, to insist on the category of the aesthetic is not to supplant the Leavisian frame of reference with a counter-model. It is to suggest only that the business of criticism lies in accommodating both scales of significance where necessary. In any such reading the force of Leavis's diagnosis would need to be accommodated.

In sum, we may say that between the too easy rhetoric of 'Under Ben Bulben' and the dramatic self-analysis of 'Among school children' there is a middle area represented by 'Byzantium' in which we can identify Leavis's personal watershed. With his intent grasp of life values in poetry, and of how they can be expressed or obfuscated, this poetic commitment to a questionable impulse is for him a mode of obfuscation. It can be accommodated to his terms only as a diagnostic symptom; which, on occasion, it may well be. In the light of this distinction, we may reconsider briefly his reading of English poetry as focused in the particular case of Milton.

Milton

Since Leavis's writing on Milton was always corrective of conventional appreciation, it is hard to say what his overall *compte rendu* would have been. He took Milton very seriously even while insisting on the mechanical and unidiomatic principle he saw in

Milton's language. He saw a passage such as the fall of Mulciber in the first book of *Paradise lost* as a moment of magical exception rather than the rule. Meanwhile, proponents of Milton will usually concede that the poem is not of equal felicity throughout. There was, therefore, a considerable grey area allowing both sides to claim a measure of victory. Hence Milton's reputation has been sufficiently modified to justify the term 'dislodged'; he is no longer casually bracketed in belle-lettrist association with Homer and Shakespeare. Yet the full intended force of Leavis's critique has been cogently answered and, as in the case of Yeats's 'Byzantium', this points to a middle ground territory, in which we can see the principled point of divergence. It should be said that Leavis's objection was in fact a double one. The mechanical imposition of authorial will was combined in Milton's verse with a damaging artificiality. Leavis would not object to artificiality as such; only as part of the overall Miltonic will. It is the second, less fundamental, objection that has been persuasively refuted, but that in turn, of course, undermines the major one.

Leavis included in his instances of Milton's damaging artificiality the description of paradise in Book IV of *Paradise lost*. Many readers felt intuitively that Milton's verse worked successfully here but were unable to give a convincing account of why it did so. For example, C. S. Lewis's *A preface to 'Paradise lost'* (1942) sought explicitly to meet Leavis's argument but it would not win over a reader genuinely troubled by Leavis's case. It is a book for the already convinced.[22] However, two later American studies gave between them a brilliant and sympathetic account of Milton's verse with special reference to the paradise theme: Louis Martz's *The paradise within* (1964) and Arnold Stein's *Answerable style* (1953). The latter especially focused on the interplay in Milton's verse between those registers, sometimes enactive ones, which evoke the world of common experience and those which, by a deliberate and literary artificiality, invoke a world not available in life. The verse is subliminally creating, beneath its immediate narrative and other functions, the central emotion of nostalgia, the yearning for the impossible, which ultimately underwrites the myth of paradise. Leavis had rightly insisted that a myth will be an empty idea if the verse cannot give it life. What these critics showed was that in the poem paradise is created from emotional experience upwards not just from a mythic idea downwards. Seen in this light, the fall of Mulciber is not an isolated moment of poetic splendour but one of the first of several strategic moments in which classical allusion

84

coupled with auditory and visual suggestion create a heart-stopping nostalgia. It stands in contrast, for example, to the thunderous and confused fall of Beelzebub at the beginning of the poem. Such an account swings the balance towards a great poem with flaws and *longeurs* rather than a largely failed poem with brilliant passages.

What is at stake in *Paradise lost*, as in 'Byzantium', is a verse mode in which the imaginative premises have only a partial, and therefore misleading, relevance to the enactive conception of poetic language. The 'immortal longings' of each poem require an aesthetic bracketing yet remain within an overall, testing dialectic with the terms of mortal life. In both cases the 'impossible' experience has somehow to be made imaginatively concrete while its poetic integrity lies in the implicit understanding of its ideal status. This is by no means a blanket vindication of the poetic mode. It merely sets out the terms for critical discrimination. But Leavis's intentness on assessing the existential values embodied in language could not accept a poetic experience so dependent on aesthetic premises of this kind.

6

The Novel, 'Maturity' and Tradition: Conrad's *The shadow line*

Leavis's work on the novel is his other area of decisive impact on the critical mapping of English literature. His effect here was even more fundamental in that criticism of the novel in English, even by the 1920s and 1930s, was not much advanced over the condition lamented by Henry James in the 1880s and 1890s. Even if the novel was now taken seriously as an artistic form, and even that could not be assumed, critics still had difficulty knowing how to talk about it. Hence Leavis's account of the English novel had a more pioneering than revisionary value and it remains the most common point of reference even for those who disagree with it.

The principal landmarks of the British novel are set out with a deliberate reductiveness signalled at the opening of *The great tradition*: Jane Austen (preceded most significantly by Samuel Richardson), George Eliot, Henry James and Joseph Conrad. Fielding, Sterne, Scott, Dickens (apart from *Hard times*) and Thackeray are among the considerable novelists set on one side. In so far as Leavis sought to his implied question 'This is so, isn't it?' the answer 'Yes, but . . .', he needed not to be disappointed in responses to *The great tradition*. The 'buts' have been many, vigorous and justified: the great tradition is not the only tradition. Yet the bold highlighting of this important line, particularly in its upward revaluation of George Eliot as an artist, rightly remains the most common point of reference. Proponents of Fielding, Sterne or Thackeray are not usually offering a substitute for Leavis's choice; only seeking to temper its exclusiveness by advancing the parallel claims of a second tradition of comic self-consciousness. His account has to that extent become canonical and it traces a tradition whose nature is peculiarly English; the terms developed for discussing the French novel, for example, would hardly suit. The French novel of the nineteenth century, with its more theoretical awareness and its more radical social rejection, lent itself to aesthetic self-consciousness. The English novel, with its underlying commitment to a positive moral and social idealism, resisted aestheticising and was correspondingly more elusive of critical focus in formal terms.

Some of the characteristic features of the English novel were summed up by D. H. Lawrence. His remark in *Lady Chatterley's lover* that 'even satire is a form of sympathy' bears on the characteristic interpenetration of artistic and 'life' values; the novelist does not stand outside the life represented. Leavis has this general point in mind when insisting that George Eliot was not capable of being a satirist.[1] And, arising from the same interpenetration, the novel was explicitly for Lawrence an instrument of psychological discovery as Leavis emphasised in his late volume, *Thought, words and creativity: art and thought in Lawrence*. This heuristic aspect became particularly salient and self-conscious in Lawrence's own work but it was a characteristic of the English novel throughout its history. When Richardson recast the seduction theme of *Pamela* into a more truthful, and tragic, form as *Clarissa* he opened up a subject-matter. The historian Christopher Hill has remarked on the accuracy and comprehensiveness of Richardson's representation of mid-eighteenth-century social forces yet it is unlikely that Richardson, if we can imagine the project, could have produced such an impersonal analysis as an enquiry in its own right. Richardson's personal conceptions were of a narrowly moralistic kind and in his greatest book we see them transcended by the dramatic logic of the material. The historical weight of *Clarissa* is a product, almost a by-product, of his intentness on his theme.[2] This sense of the novel as a mode of discovering its own subject-matter runs through the English tradition and the relative lack of preoccupation with 'aesthetic' issues was an aspect of its heuristic flexibility.

Leavis, as we have seen, was peculiarly aware of the creative, heuristic dimension of literary form. He understood it not just as an abstract premiss, as it were, anterior to the work but as an active struggle of the artist to bring the material to a focus of understanding; a struggle which is in some sense re-enacted in every fully responsive reading of the work. But the achievement of form is not in itself necessarily the achievement of significance. The actual form may reflect failure or avoidance of the creative struggle. Leavis was concerned with the production of significance, the nature and genesis of meaning, in the literary context. It is this eye to the quick of the creative struggle that Leavis brought to the reading of the English novel. Hence his reading has remained one of the most penetrating accounts we have while resisting extrapolation as a generalised 'approach' to the novel at large.

The point is worth pausing on. In his best criticism Leavis's understanding of creativity amounts to a creative activity in its own right. It is sometimes said that all critical appreciation is a second order of creativity: it erects an adjacent structure from which the primary one can be viewed. If this is so we should distinguish the sense in which this applies to a critic of Leavis's quality. Several commentators have observed that Leavis is the notable exception to T. S. Eliot's dictum, later modified in fact, that the important original literary critics were all creative artists in their own right. Eliot's point, which is a shrewd one in many instances, was that critics may infuse an otherwise frustrated creativity into their reading. But drawing on the earlier discussion of 'sincerity' and 'impersonality', I would rather say that Leavis is not merely the exception to Eliot's generalisation but the precise counter-case to its underlying principle. His best criticism is most personal, and inimitable, in its impersonality. It is his ability to give himself to the work, putting his own sense of creative possibility at its disposal, that gives the force and authority to critical statements which, at another level, do not seem to be saying very much and may even seem quite empty when taken in isolation. Keats's version of artistic impersonality was phrased as 'negative capability' and we might give the phrase a further twist in this context by saying that true creativeness in criticism is shown by knowing exactly when to stop.

All this is to suggest the quality in Leavis that made him a peculiarly fruitful reader of the English novel. Yet he came to an appreciation of the novel comparatively late in his career and had to work out his way of addressing long narrative fictions after having practised the close analysis of poetry. No doubt F.R.L's interest in the novel was influenced by Q.D.L's long-standing critical involvement with it and that is commemorated by their joint authorship of *Dickens the novelist*. But the actual process of adjustment for Leavis himself is more significantly reflected in the earlier book on Lawrence and in *The great tradition. D. H. Lawrence: novelist* was based on a series of *Scrutiny* essays and used as its central formula 'the novel as dramatic poem'; a phrase which

suggestively indicates Leavis's personal way into the novel in so far
as he needed to give his reading a conceptual focus. Whatever the
immediate personal or tactical value of the phrase, it is interesting
that he should have conceptualised the novel as a poem for this
throws light in turn on his sense of a poem; and, indeed, of literature at large. And it is worth noting in passing that the gradual
process of adjustment registered by the difference between the
pamphlet on Lawrence published in 1930 and *D. H. Lawrence:
novelist*, or by the late book on Dickens as opposed to the dismissal
of most of his *œuvre* in *The great tradition*, reflects what has been said
of the English novel itself. Its true power does not lie in its most
evident and conscious properties such as the moralism of
Richardson, the sentiment and grotesquerie of Dickens, or the
explicit doctrines of Lawrence. But the underlying point here is
that the public process of Leavis's adjustment to the novel has an
analytic value for us with respect to his reading of literature at
large. For his confrontation with fiction enforced an even more
urgent focus on the nature of 'literary' significance.

Leavis himself usually dismissed the view that different literary
genres require a corresponding difference of 'approach'. And in so
far as this bears on a possible source of academic mystification and
an avoidance of critical issues, this seems to me to be a good
tactical principle. Yet the evidence summarised in the preceding
paragraph suggests that prose fiction did indeed require some
adjustment of attention or discourse even for him. If there is some
possible equivocation here it is encapsulated in the very phrase
'novel as dramatic poem' in that the significance of conflating
these genres is dependent on their assumed distinction. I propose,
therefore, to conclude this chapter with a close examination of this
phrase but first I wish to consider the earlier development of this
conception in *The great tradition* and its detailed use in a particular
essay.

The great tradition

I have suggested that *The great tradition* is an attempted 'mapping'
of the English novel. To convey the nature of Leavis's reading this
metaphor would have to imply at least a contour map showing the
eminences, lowlands and watersheds. Indeed, the appropriate
image is really of a guide able to place you at strategic points on the
terrain itself so as to demonstrate its immediate texture within a

larger view. The part is seen through the whole and the whole through the part to create a sense of scale and representativeness as well as immediate quality. But apart from its intrinsic exemplary interest the progress of his argument throws light on his conception of fiction.

It has been suggested, notably by Edward Greenwood, that *The great tradition* sits a little uneasily between a classical 'mimetic' view and the romantic 'expressive' view espoused in the Lawrence book.[3] My remarks so far on the 'creative' exploration of experience have already tended to dissolve this dichotomy. We have already seen that for Leavis 'mimesis' is not just the literalistic reflection of an outer world but an analogical enactive process within the language. Although this is more readily identifiable in a local way in poetry it has an equivalent in the sympathetic activity of the novelist. Hence the structure of *The great tradition* reflects this dissolution of 'mimesis' and 'expression' as a positive aspect of its conception of fiction. For the differences between George Eliot, James and Conrad, while explaining the difference of emphasis to which Greenwood refers, actually highlight, I would say, the underlying unity of Leavis's conception. The development of his argument is not so much a mature of models as a unitary recognition clarified and reinforced by the very different writers to whom it is addressed.

I have referred to the 'structure' of *The great tradition* and it has indeed a boldness of outline that helps explain the reductiveness with which it has sometimes been read, but Leavis's method is one for which his own term 'organic' is more appropriate. On occasion, for example, he eschews his author's chronology to pursue a particular comparative theme and then has to double back. The effect of this is not to pick up a loose thread but to modify the pattern of a continuous one. If the image of weaving suggests itself here, we might say that the apparent simplicity of his 'warp' is transformed by the delicacy of his weft. Within a clear sense of ultimate direction the detailed process of argument is a constant sideways movement building up a many-layered and relative awareness. The meaning of the individual comment is conditioned by its place in a complex set of comparisons. Leavis's reputation for peremptory approval or dismissal of authors has its basis in his trenchancy of expression but it is ironic in that his method constantly insists on the conditional, or perspectival, meaning of the judgement.

Hence in his opening chapter he makes summary reference to

many novelists not to be discussed in the body of the work. Yet in some cases, such as Fielding and Scott, he acknowledges both an intrinsic and an historical importance in them. This relative aspect of his judgements, left largely undeveloped in this opening section, becomes crucial in his chapters on Eliot, James and Conrad for in all three cases the supreme achievement he sets out to define goes with severe limitations. More to the point, the achievement is shown to be intimately related to the limitations. Artistic success is understood as a winning out over potential failures of grasp and integrity. As Heidegger noted in a passage quoted earlier (p. 45), the strong claim made for creative literature cannot be predicated on a general category of the 'poetic' but only on significant achievement within this. And even within individual writers or works, Leavis uses the negative to define the positive. He focuses on the artistic struggle, and the issues at stake in it, rather than offer either general judgements or a critical accounting of credit and debit. In this way the uniqueness and experiential weight of the work in question emerge, as he would say, 'irresistibly', in the reading. Of course, once the judgement is formulated it may become a piece of 'portable property' for others but that is not the spirit of its production. And this same relational awareness governs his use of 'mimetic' or 'expressive' terms as his argument progresses through Eliot, James and Conrad.

The originality of his reading of Eliot lies in challenging the then common view that her fiction struggles under the weight of an unassimilated philosophical and didactic intelligence. He demonstrates that her weakness lies rather in her moments of personal emotional identification, as with Dorothea Brooke and Maggie Tulliver. Once again, his diagnostic criteria here are impersonality and the dissolution of such dualistic categories as 'thought' and 'feeling' in the act of creative understanding. The centrepiece of his discussion is an extended comparison between Gwendolen Harleth, in *Daniel Deronda*, and Isabel Archer in James's *The portrait of a lady*. Here he draws on the Englishness and the femaleness of Eliot as compared with the American and male perception of James. If asked for a piece of writing exemplifying the importance of criticism, and of literature, for Leavis, or indeed for anyone, this comparison, with its specificity of demonstration and its range of implication, would provide as good an example as one could wish. I will make two particular points about it here.

The first is a parenthetical one concerning the difference between the male and the female writer. This is a matter that exercised Leavis as indeed it must exercise any serious reader of the English novel. It was also a major theme of Q. D. Leavis's reading of the novel. Yet for neither of them was it separated off as *the* theme; as the only, or the fundamental, clue. Now that critical attention has, very profitably, been focused on this and related questions the Leavises' treatment of this whole domain may repay attention precisely because it is an aspect of their holistic critical account.

But my major point concerns the characteristically comparative method Leavis adopts. In drawing on *The portrait of a lady* Leavis invokes what he considers to be the strongest work of another major writer so that a proper sense of proportion is, as it were, built in to the discussion. He is also drawing on a work with a manifest sense of artistic control; the quality that James, and others, had felt George Eliot to lack. Hence when he goes on to show how much Eliot actually gets into the Gwendolen story as compared with what James gets in to the Isabel story, we are made to recognise the *artistic* power of Eliot. An old schoolteacher of mine used to appeal to the phrase 'the art that conceals art' as a universal critical nostrum. The phrase is not an enlightening one but the problem it covers over is real enough. There are certain kinds of wholeness in which the overt signs of complexity disappear by being so completely absorbed. This is always a difficult achievement to account for critically. It usually requires the creation of a pertinent sense of context or comparison yet that can in itself become a distraction. One of Leavis's important abilities was to identify this kind of wholeness as distinguished from mere simplicity on the one hand or an apparent complexity on the other. He had this ability because it was the nerve centre of his whole anti-Cartesian endeavour. Hence, in his discussion of the Gwendolen story Leavis affirms the category of art even as it disappears into an inclusive and maturely impersonal understanding of experience. That, I believe, is the positive achievement of the chapter and readers should not be distracted from it by his suggestion, towards the end, that this story could be extracted as a separate novel. I have myself always understood that as a rhetorical way of making his point although Leavis did entertain it, for a while, as a literal possibility. It is a final suggestion made to point up the argument; it is not the point of the argument.

Having used James as an analytic means to define what resists analysis in Eliot, Leavis moves on to consider James in his own right and as he does so there is a characteristic, relational shift in his terms which Leavis actually draws to our attention. James's consciously artistic concern is the condition of his achievement but also the root of its ambivalence for Leavis. Hence Leavis first modifies the focus from 'art' to the 'poetic' to bring out the positive nature of James's vision; its penetrative and organising power as a kind of heightened mimesis. He is not contradicting anything he said in the Eliot chapter and yet he effects a subtle, seismic shift in his frame of reference. He speaks elsewhere of critical language as a 'constant adjustment' and he means by this something more fundamental than a readiness to qualify a point. Adequate response to a literary vision involves recognising its possible challenge to habitual terms and in the present instance his adjustment allows him to give full weight to the nature of James's conception as distinct from Eliot's.

He then proceeds to the negative side of James's artistic self-consciousness which is evident for him in the three major late novels *The wings of the dove* (1902), *The ambassadors* (1903) and *The golden bowl* (1905). All three are vitiated, for him, by a kind of decadence. He sees in them an over-attention to the 'doing' which actually obscures the nature of what is being done; even, in some measure, from James himself. The interesting feature of this analysis for present purposes is Leavis's concentration on James's prose which, in the late phase, loses its sinuous strength to become an endless self-qualification. Obliquity has become so habitual, in Leavis's view, that the subject is hardly there at all. It is worth remarking that Leavis's own prose style suffered a comparable fate in his later years. Both men had reason to feel they had failed to find, or create, a significant audience and, whatever the differences between them, this may be a common factor in their increased tendency to self-communing. If that is so then just as *The portrait of a lady* indicates the proper strength of the Jamesian manner, so *The great tradition* exemplifies the confident combination of delicacy and force in Leavis's best critical prose. But Leavis's analysis of James's late manner attributed it to a quite different cause; a failure of 'life' on James's part whereby his artistic concern, unlike George Eliot's, became too much an end in itself. Leavis, by this point in his argument, is indeed concentrating on the 'expressive' means to the detriment of the 'mimetic' complexity of *The golden bowl*. He suggests, for example, that as readers we wish Charlotte and the Prince to live out their passion honestly. This suggestion is intended to pinpoint James's failure to give proper weight to passional life. But in the novel James is

93

is careful to suggest the flawed quality of their relationship. Leavis's reading of *The golden bowl* is another revelatory instance in which his summative existential judgement illuminates without fully encompassing the work in question. But if we are concerned at this point with his terms and criteria, rather than the specific judgements, then his attention is still on the creative relation of 'art' to 'experience'. The mutuality of 'mimesis' and 'expression' remains the implicit criterion even for the occasion on which it appears not be satisfactorily realised.

As Leavis moves on to Conrad, there is a further development of the shift already noted in the transition from Eliot to James. With Conrad he continues to emphasise the 'poetic' principle in the vision, and composition, of the novels. And the point is even more crucial in Conrad's case since his method is not so essentially dependent on the inward notation of consciousness found in Eliot and James. Indeed, some of Conrad's most successful novels, such as *The secret agent* and *Victory*, have a strong element of deliberate melodrama and even *Nostromo*, his masterpiece, works through dramatic personalities akin to those of Elizabethan and Jacobean drama. Hence, in the course of discussing such different writers as Eliot, James and Conrad, Leavis has modified his emphasis, but this is a change of focus rather than a change in the instrument. The 'mimetic' and the 'expressive' remain complementary aspects of the 'poetic'. The 'poetic' is a process of recognition or discovery that encompasses and uses mimesis.

This underlying conception is borne out by the two subsequent books on Lawrence and Dickens in which Leavis moves back from a modern to a Victorian writer. The earlier progress from Eliot through James and Conrad to Lawrence was a shift towards the modern and that is indeed a part explanation of the increasing emphasis on the poetic method. But the same 'poetic' conception is crucial to the Dickens book, too, which suggests that this conception should not be identified with just one of its aspects. Indeed, it is precisely a resolution of such antinomies: 'art' *is* 'mature understanding'; the 'poetic' is where 'reality' and ''sincerity' are mutually necessary terms.

The case of Dickens is especially significant in this connection. The Leavises shared the general obtuseness, as we can now see it, about Dickens which persisted well after Edmund Wilson's seminal essay in *The wound and the bow* (1941); although few can claim to have made such amends as is offered by *Dickens the novelist*.[4] What is interesting in the present context is that Dickens is a substantial off-stage presence even in *The great tradition*; not least as an influence on James and Conrad. And the way he is introduced is for such features as the poetic transformation of melodrama. In other words, if Leavis had wished to rewrite *The great tradition* in the light of his later view of Dickens he would have had to make curiously little change to the text. The changes would be major in the sense that the minus signs would become pluses; that is to say qualifying phrases would be removed. But the essential presence and shape of Dickens is already largely there. With hindsight, therefore, it is understandable that Leavis came to recognise the richness of poetic organisation in Dickens and to see it as a form of moral understanding. We might say that the two greatest practitioners of the Victorian novel remained for a long time *artistically* invisible. Eliot was a 'moralist' and Dickens an 'entertainer'; a literary equivalent of Sleary in *Hard times*. Leavis's achievement was to reveal artistry as a quality of understanding supremely present where least noticed.

Leavis's three books on the novel are a highly sophisticated identification of the 'artistic' and the 'moral'. Their sophistication lies partly in the way the inescapable dualisms of our habitual discourse are set against the recognitions enabled by the works themselves. As Heidegger saw, the holistic recognitions of poetry are belied by the Cartesian categories implicit in almost any analytic parlance available to us. Leavis's commentary allows the text to do its job while showing us where and how to look. The blend of simplicity and sophistication in his own discourse gives it something of the apparently unassuming force of the writers he admires. George Eliot at her best *seems* simpler than James. There is an analogous artistry in Leavis's capacity to cut through to the essential with apparently simple strokes.

All this is to suggest something of the underlying conception that animates Leavis's reading of fiction and it places the essential burden once again on his specific tactics and rhetoric. Having indicated the general method of *The great tradition* I propose to look at the detailed presentation of a particular essay in which, as it happens, the mutuality of the moral and the artistic occurs within a peculiarly fruitful concentration of Leavisian themes.

'Maturity' and *The shadow line*

I have noted that the 'enactive' use of language in poetry has an equivalent for Leavis in the sympathetic activity of the novelist and it is indicative that a key focal term for Leavis's criticism of the novel was 'maturity'; as opposed to 'sincerity' with respect to poetry. This is not an absolute distinction, of course; the poetic emotions of both Shelley and Auden were immature in Leavis's view. But the shift in genre does seem to involve a difference, if not in approach, then in the emphasis implied by the key terms. And whereas the word 'sincerity' was adapted by Leavis to become a kind of honorary technical term, the word 'maturity' retains all the problematic openness of its common usage. This perhaps reflects the shift towards a closer interpenetratation of art and experience as identified in the English novel. And in assessing the experiential weight of the word 'maturity', I will consider in turn what Leavis means to invoke by the related term 'tradition'. For the fact that some of the key figures in the great tradition are not English allows for a sharper focus on its nature. All these issues are raised in the lecture on *The shadow line*.[5]

As with the Yeats lecture, this is a late piece returning to an author on whom Leavis had expressed his judgement some twenty years previously. He, therefore, addresses the occasion with an initial note of embarrassment at having apparently nothing new to say. But in fact both the sense of occasion and the sense of having nothing new to say are intrinsic, and characteristic, in the critical statement he goes on to make. It seems that he was invited to give a lecture on Conrad and considered this version as delivered rather an unfinished draft. There is indeed too much late Leavisian self-communing in the lecture which revision might have reduced. But this enables us to see the elements in his thought process in some ways the more clearly. And at a more structural level the remarkable quality of the lecture is the economy and authority with which it makes its general case while using an apparently ramshackle assemblage of adventitious materials. As it turns out, these adventitious references have a multi-layered and mutually supportive significance for his critical case as it unfolds. The difficulty of getting started, which Leavis noted in the Yeats lecture, is tackled here through a series of third objects. The principal steps of his argument are as follows.

He opens by noting that his earlier assessment of Conrad has not essentially changed (p. 92). He then mentions a symposium on 'Joseph Conrad today' in a recent volume of *The London Magazine*. From this he picks out a remark by John Wain on the good fortune of the English in being the beneficiaries of Conrad's 'choice' of language (p. 93). Having used Wain's journalistic sally to develop his own opposed conception of Conrad's naturalisation into English, Leavis raises the question of where Conrad's real strengths lie. And he finds wanting as guides in this respect the well-known comments of E. M. Forster and Virginia Woolf (p. 96). He then adduces another symposium contributor, Mr Tom Hopkinson, for a representative view of Conrad's *œuvre* as consisting of tales of nautical virtue manifested in conditions of, often melodramatic, adversity (p. 98). This provides Leavis with his positive project in the lecture. He wishes to distinguish that quality in Conrad which transcends the nautical terms of reference and which is not open to the objection of melodramatic or rhetorical inflation. For this purpose, now a third of the way into the lecture, he adduces *The shadow line*. He offers it as representative of Conrad's true genius and appeals to the essentially 'poetic' nature of Conrad's method; a generic emphasis which is to run through the remainder of the lecture (p. 100). He only now introduces the term 'maturity' which provides a complementary focus for the following discussion; although a conceptually elusive one in that it cannot apparently be defined in terms other than those of the story itself (p. 100). These two threads of generic definition and moral attestation are united in a culminating definition of the tale as 'dramatic poem' (p. 109). He ends on a comparison with *Silas Marner* as another considerable work by a major novelist within a minor compass.

Even in this mechanical summary, it is evident that Leavis is moving from several casual starting-points to a recognition of Conrad's achievement couched in a principled and universal way. The question is how the positive latter half of the essay benefits from, or is conditioned by, the opening section. It may be that Leavis is warming up his audience by hitting a few convenient targets and performing a sufficient public service in doing so. There is some truth in that, but this opening section, as I have suggested, also serves to define the critical theme in more positive ways.

The first point to make here is that the series of occasional references supplies him eventually with a vehicle for his own statement while removing as far as possible the necessity for an 'original' argument. He can work towards a general statement from a relative starting-point. For his criticism highlights a fundamental difficulty of literary commentary which can be expressed logically but has to be addressed rhetorically. Most typically he does not wish to occupy new, or non-obvious, ground and the point on which he does wish to stand is not essentially amenable to extended argument. He wishes to show the work forth in its self-evidence and, to that extent, every elaboration of argument is an implicit undermining of what he wishes to show. Hence there is a sense in which his critical procedure answers to Cleveland's image 'Motion, as in a Mill /Is busie standing still'. In the present instance, he constructs the significance, as opposed to the meaning, of his positive recognition by a series of negations. The elaborations of 'meaning' can actually obfuscate 'significance' in the apprehension of a work. Where many commentators assume 'significance' while expounding on 'meaning', Leavis focuses almost exclusively on the issue of significance. His method here is to set up a reverse spiral by which to home in with increasing precision on what he takes the significance of Conrad's tale to be.

This deliberate circularity can be seen particularly in the use of a term like 'maturity'. The word is problematic because it is at once too empty of specific meaning while being ideologically loaded. It carries, we might say, the maximum evaluative charge with the minimum of agreed, identifiable reference. One of the essential and repeated objections to Leavis is that he imposes his own moral vocabulary on the works he reads. Who is Leavis, or any one else, to tell us what is truly 'mature'? Can such a vocabulary be used at all in a critical context? The same problem was there, of course, with the term 'sincerity' but in that case Leavis had sought to define it as a locally demonstrable quality of the text. 'Maturity' here seems a more unmediated attestation of value as we might perhaps expect in the less readily adducible context of an extended prose fiction. And this is not just a matter of length. The realist novel is no more intrinsically tendentious than any other literary form but it is perhaps more insidiously so in view of its wide readership, its socially critical purpose and its mimetic immediacy. Hence the special emphasis on the novel in the doyen of Marxist critics, Georg Lukács, and in many of his successors. The problem that has been raised with the term 'maturity', then, is whether it is a purely ideological construct reflecting a particular set of moral and social values or whether it has some legitimately universal or objectifiable meaning. For Leavis, that would be a false antithesis arising from an inadequate sense of language. In this respect the disagreement surrounding the use of this term epitomises the incommensurability of Leavis's humanism and almost the whole range of political, psychoanalytical and linguistic discourses that have characterised much published academic literary commentary in the mid to late years of this century; what Paul Ricoeur has called 'the hermeneutics of suspicion'.[6]

I have already indicated in a previous chapter that the general threshold for recognising ideological construction in apparently 'natural' or 'moral' terms is much lower than at the time of Leavis's greatest influence and that is in itself an important gain. A term like 'maturity' does need to be looked at with a pertinently skilled care. But in so far as merely conventional responses are dangerous, the danger now lies in the supposition that a word such as 'maturity' has no value at all; other than a diagnostic one with regard to its user. I wish rather to suggest that the 'hermeneutics of suspicion', far from disposing of Leavisian usage, put us in a position to consider it more testingly and appreciatively. This is not to say that it clears up the problem but that it allows us to see the nature of the problem more clearly.

What is at stake here is whether Leavis has something important to say for which the use of this word is necessary and whether, in using it, he is appropriately aware of the relative nature of his discourse. It seems to me that he is so aware and that the justification of the term in use is bound up with this awareness. Such meanings are not just inertly contained, or uncritically adduced, in the discourse: they are precisely the ideal end to which the artistic and critical discourses are directed both separately and in combination. The ultimate, or noumenal, ideality of the end is not necessarily disabling therefore; it is simply the recognised condition. 'Maturity' is not just an assumed significance, it is the locus of struggle towards a significance. What underwrites the usage is the whole posture of the critical discourse which is to set up a symbiosis between the work and its commentary.

The paragraph in which the word 'maturity' is first introduced exemplifies this broader interrelation of text and commentary:

The ship and command are, for the young captain, a symbol and a test: the experience in the gulf of Siam is an ordeal, a kind of *rite de passage*; these things are plain, and indeed, explicit. But the maturity with which he emerges from the ordeal is an immensely more subtle matter than anything suggested by the idea of the Master Mariner, by proof now worthy of the Red Ensign and its traditions. For the novelist recalling and recreating the experience the maturity in question is that of the whole man as he was himself, conscious of complex potentialities and subtle demands on life. (p. 100)

Before moving to the substantive issues raised by this paragraph, it is worth noting that the opening lines provide a parenthetical hint concerning the nature of reading. Later in the lecture Leavis explicitly refrains from elaborating any symbolic pattern in the work, yet here he refers to the young man's ship and command as a 'symbol'. The word as used here is precisely not a literary term and the implication of enhanced significance arises quite naturally because it refers to the captain's *own* perception of this significance; it is not just attributed directly to the ship. The word 'symbol', we might say, is a way of referring to a perceived significance, not a technical means for producing one.[7] We could take this as an effective definition of how symbolic meaning is to be seen in the tale itself. For Leavis does not actually dismiss this aspect later on even while he carefully sets it aside from his discussion. He implies that this is partly owing to shortage of time but the priority the decision implies is characteristic.

Symbolism is a proper way of pointing up significance by an author and therefore by a critic. But the explication of symbolism may well short-circuit the inwardness of attention from which the recognition of its significance arises. Leavis sees in the literary text a significantly posed gesture towards the reader's three-dimensional world of experience. Explication of symbolism often focuses our attention on the two-dimensional literary mechanism of the text and loses the holistic, bi-focal attention required for fully responding to it. From the young captain's point of view, the significance of the occasion is created both by its objective 'grammar' (he *is* the captain, it *is* his first command) and by the seriousness and openness with which he undertakes it. Likewise as we in turn respond to the captain as a literary object, significance arises both from the specific construction on the page and from our adequacy of response. It is this latter, elusive factor that Leavis seeks to exemplify in his own reading. Hence his constant vigilance to prevent significance being reified into literary symbolism. His effort is to keep the horizontal and vertical dimensions of reading in simultaneous focus. Of course, the reflections I have extrapolated here from his use of the term 'symbol' are not intended to imply that this was his meaning at this point. But they indicate how his choice of vocabulary, and his tactical priorities, denote a precise and considered traffic between text and commentary. Just as he leaned *on* the moral term 'sincerity' so we see him leaning *against* the literary term 'symbol'. Neither word is either pro-scribed or uncritically adduced. The critical rhetoric, as he said, is a 'constant adjustment'.

That is the point of view from which to consider the principal burden of this paragraph more closely. Leavis moves, within three short sentences, from the narrative content of the tale to the imaginative means, and finally to the artist himself. Leavis treats these three orders as a continuum and there are hints in the tale and its subtitle that the first-person narration in this case repre-sents something of a dramatised confession. But Leavis, as we have seen in his discussion of Yeats, is characteristically ready to read the experience of the work in a pretty direct relation to the author and that is an important aspect of the present lecture. Hence, the first use of the word 'maturity' refers simply to the young captain while in the final sentence it refers to Conrad's own experience which he is 'recalling and recreating' *as* the captain's. And in culminating this movement the third sentence has a charac-teristically Leavisian formulation in which total meaning and total vacuity are dangerously allied: 'the whole man, as he was himself, conscious of complex potentialities and subtle demands on life'. Taken in isolation particularly, these asseverative phrases seem not so much meaningless as empty. I have suggested that some items of the characteristically Leavisian vocabulary, such as 'creative' or 'sincerity' are underwritten by a specifically evolved meaning. But the adjectival gestures of 'complex' and 'subtle' in this sentence only draw attention to what seems a blank cheque we are being asked to endorse. There is undoubtedly a problem of articulacy here for Leavis and this is the kind of crucial moment in which we see his prose succumb to the burden it attempts to carry. But there is a real burden and in the present instance he communi-cates his meaning more effectively than might be supposed from dwelling on these phrases in isolation. For in moving to Conrad's own maturity as the analogue of the captain's, Leavis is drawing on an earlier part of the lecture, the full import of which was not previously apparent.

One of his isolated comments before settling in to the discussion of *The shadow line* was his critique of John Wain's hapless reference to Conrad's adoption of the English language as a matter of 'choice'.

In attracting an artist as big as Conrad, we, the English, had a stroke of luck. But of course it was more than luck. We had, in those days, the reputation of being a good audience, intelligent and serious enough to deserve the best that a great author could do. Have we still got that reputation? Would a modern Conrad still make that choice? (p. 93)

The criticism Leavis makes of this exemplifies his concern for linguistic responsibility as noted earlier. Wain's reference to Conrad's 'choice' might be understood as a metaphorical shorthand for the way in which Conrad came to write in English. But the effect of the term is to produce a mildly chauvinistic glow for which any note of irony, along with the final rhetorical questions, acts as an excuse rather than a control. Leavis is effectively diagnosing the mode of thought and feeling out of which Wain's comment arises. That is the insidious fluency which Leavis's style seeks assiduously to avoid. Leavis goes on to make his own opposed point by a telling use of quotation from Conrad himself:

The merest idea of choice never entered my head. And as to adoption — well, yes, there was adoption; but it was I who was adopted by the genius of the language.

But this quotation is not there just as a corrective to John Wain. It enables Leavis to establish an important complex of meanings through Conrad's own words. And in the light of what has been said concerning Leavis's near vacuity and Wain's insidious fluency, we might comment on Conrad's crucial phrase 'the genius of the language' which could also be seen as an empty formula. The appropriate comment here is Leslie Stephen's remark, quoted by Queenie Leavis, on those who had objected to Matthew Arnold's formula, 'poetry is a criticism of life'. It has, he says, been 'much ridiculed by some writers who were apparently unable to distinguish between an epigram and a philosophical dogma'.[8]

Conrad's phrase is a synoptic way of referring to a complex of recognitions about the individuality of this particular national tradition as inscribed in its language. As with Leavis's use of 'sincerity' or 'creative', the phrase appeals to a body of experience rather than defines a single idea. Indeed, Conrad's phrase bears on the whole relation of the individual to an historical tradition; 'tradition' being another word in which the conceptual counter is notoriously inadequate to the complex of experience invoked. In effect, the early part of the lecture is devoted to developing the personal experience of belonging to a tradition; and in particular to a tradition that the individual has consciously joined. This is, of course, the situation of Conrad's young captain.

The crucial distinction in the tale is between a merely dutiful, acquiescent observance of the traditional rules of conduct and the more complex, indeterminable relation of independence which Leavis is defining by contrast as fully mature. This is not to belittle the value, or the difficulty, of applying the inherited forms in the immediate, changing circumstances of life; whether as a ship's captain or as a minor novelist. But to recognise the need for creative departure from precedent is to possess the inherited understanding in a very complete way. Leavis's favoured formulation that 'we do not belong' just to ourselves catches the sense of obligation below the level of personal 'choice'. Moral conduct by definition implies some value beyond the self. And whatever the complexities of circumstance, interpretation, etc., there comes every so often a point on fundamental issues at which the individual's moral choice lies in the recognition that there is no choice. And it is no paradox that habitual respect for the impersonality of tradition acts as a preparation for those moments when the impersonal imperative is actually to break with it. The young captain encounters such a moment when he decides to take the sick first mate on board and as Leavis notes parenthetically of *The secret sharer*, elaborating the same line of thought, the young captain of that tale similarly feels he has no choice but to rescue his countryman condemned for a self-confessed homicide. This is, of course, the manner in which Conrad perceived his adoption by the English language and his subsequent modification of its forms; particularly the novel form. This was not a 'choice' so much as a recognition.

In effect, the paragraph I initially quoted is the moment of transition in the lecture from an extended discussion of Conrad at large to a discussion of the specific tale during which the underlying subject, the nature of tradition, actually remains the same. In the light of that it is worth noting the more immediate context of the transition. Leavis has invoked E. M. Forster's comments on the lack of a philosophical view at the heart of Conrad's rhetoric. He wishes to reverse the implication of Forster's point by seeing this as precisely the condition of a creative understanding. In Leavis's subsequent account, it is made clear that the tale neither started in, nor terminates as, a 'meaning'. As Leavis puts it a little later, we learn how 'to read it when we become aware of the nature of its concern for significance' (p. 103). Its concern, in other words, is of a more fundamental kind than Forster's summary account allows for. It is a questioning, and affirmation, of the nature of significance for a given individual; a concern very close, of course, to Leavis's own central preoccupation in the reading of literature.

In going on to call the tale a dramatic poem, Leavis means that its narrative and propositional elements are the vehicle for something more. That something is not a vague afflatus but a controlled investigation of the experience of significance. A poem is creative in its use of the known to discover the unknown. Hence Leavis's way of moving from his initial demurral at Forster's implication is to place himself increasingly at the quick of the creative purpose underlying the tale. Touching on Hopkinson's essay he says:

> When I read this account of Conrad I thought of *The Shadow Line*. It is central to his genius, and it might have been written to facilitate the refutation of such an account. Having made this last suggestion I withdraw it — or withdraw that way of making the point: *The Shadow Line* is clearly something Conrad *had* to write. (p. 99)

There is a kind of tactical sub-text to this. He suggests a speculative genesis for the tale and then withdraws it, or half withdraws it, because it falsifies the nature of the creative conception. As with the matter of writing in English, that process is not one of choice as normally understood. But the effect of making the speculative suggestion which is withdrawn, but not actually removed, is like a species of metaphor in its non-logical precision. It serves to place us in a prior, creative standpoint *vis-à-vis* the now finished work. In the strict logic of his argument this is not necessary at all, yet for understanding the impact of his reading it is highly indicative. Without claiming to know what creative purpose or understanding actually underlay the genesis of the tale, Leavis reads it, almost instinctively it seems, from the creative point of view; from the imagined viewpoint of its not yet existing. He then goes on to argue the close identity of the young captain with Conrad himself as the creative and questioning voice in the tale; an identification which underlies the ready conflation of author's and character's experience in the paragraph quoted. Without invoking an authorial intention, which would be critically irrelevant even if it could be known, Leavis reads the tale in terms of the author's creative struggle. As Heidegger believed we are culturally deadened to the nature of Being even when practising philosophy, so in respect of literature we can be deadened to the nature of significance. Reading in the way he does, Leavis is not commandeering the author's function after the event, but he is attending to the most fundamental genesis of meaning which every completed work may to some extent efface. His rhetorical tactic here reflects the way in which he puts a creative intuition at the service of the work.

Hence the paragraph quoted as being so questionable when considered in isolation is to be understood rather as a conduit by which the implications developed in the early part of the lecture are being directed, still in a gestural or promissory way, towards the tale itself. The significance of the tale can only be fully appreciated in the light of 'extra-literary' significances such as those already sketched. Just as Leavis's vocabulary, in its 'constant adjustment', effects a considered interaction of literary and non-literary implication, so the structure of the lecture sets up the extra-literary frame of reference which proves in the event not to be separable. His strategy has invoked the inward complexity of 'choice' before identifying its thematic importance to the tale. Leavis typically creates his frame of reference as a way of proposing the fundamental significance pertinent to the work. The art of this lies in the way it is not merely 'background', or the 'material' the artist has used, and which the critic is externally adducing. It is always perceived as an integral aspect of the work; perhaps because 'work' in this context is understood more as a verb than as a noun. And correspondingly in his language of commentary phrases like 'complex potentialities' and 'subtle demands on life', or words like 'maturity', are largely gestural. In so far as these expressions are going to achieve a definition it will be by an imaginative identification with Conrad's own struggle to provide it.[9]

It has already become apparent that the ideal act of commentary for Leavis would be a reading of the text which indeed he places at the centre of his Yeats lecture and, by exhortation, it is the culmination of the Conrad lecture too. But, of course, this ideal vanishing-point of criticism is not a literal intent so much as an informing spirit of the critical rhetoric and it applies not just on the explicit occasions, such as the exhortation to reread the work, it is implied pervasively in the fundamental vocabulary. In so far as 'maturity' is not actually Conrad's term, it invokes a standard brought to the tale by the critic. Yet the effective function of this very open, if not to say bland, term is to refer us back to the work, and in turn to the Conradian experience focused in the work, to determine its significance. It may seem paradoxical to say that the strength of his criticism lies in the weakness of its central terms but that is, I believe, his essential, if not necessarily conscious, posture. The term has a gestural purpose and a categorial meaning, there is a function for the critic, but on inspection its non-intrusion on the work is an important aspect of its meaning. Perhaps Wittgenstein's famous remark at the end of the *Tractatus*, about his own argument being like a ladder to be kicked away when the point has been grasped, may be invoked here. It is the necessary, yet provisional, term for seeing the work from the right angle. In so far as the term has a specific force for us this lies more in what it takes from the work than in what it brings to it.

Leavis's discourse characteristically seeks to combine an ostensive effect with an evaluative commentary; it also seeks to combine a sense of creative indeterminacy with clarity of analysis. This entails a care not just for the meaning of his terms but for their moment-to-moment status; a care that gives his discourse its implicit theoretical poise. As has been observed, the strains of this often show and sometimes he turns this to account in a demonstrative way as in the 'erasure' effect just noted once again in his way of adducing *The shadow line* in response to Hopkinson. Or more simply as in this instance:

> It is part of a complex process of evocation and what I will call poetic definition, by which the idea and the sense of a world or realm of values — is that the right word? not really, but I use it for brevity — are conveyed. (p. 105)

What is 'conveyed' here is a gesture enacting the felt inadequacy, the thematically pertinent inadequacy as it happens, of any particular verbal formulation to the recognition in question.[10] Whether or not the import of the phrase 'realm of values' *could* be adequately rendered, the point, we feel, is ultimately self-evident or it is incommunicable and the prose constantly hovers between these possibilities; or else it attempts to superimpose them; or again, as in the present instance, it foregrounds the difficulty as in itself a way of reflecting on the work. Hence such moments occur alongside directly affirmative forms such as 'potently communicated to us' or 'brought home to us with great potency'. In view of the strong personal stamp of his criticism, it is as well to note the constitutive modesty, as it were, of his discourse. Highly wilful cerebrations can be couched in a rhetoric of modest disclaimer and collegial civility. Leavis's critical authority is bound up with the way he respects the limits of his own discourse.

This capacity to give himself to the work rather than impose himself on it may partly explain the effect in his criticism of being disposable when read. I believe I am not alone in finding that his critical case, where it is convincing, tends typically to survive in memory as a formulated attitude, as a deepened perception of the work, rather than as an elaborated argument or interpretation. What I have been highlighting in the lecture on *The shadow line* is the way in which a field of interrelated significances is set up which seems inadequately formulated, or merely asserted, at any single moment yet which comes increasingly to bear as a whole. Michael Black, who worked for one of Leavis's publishers and therefore needed to assess the prose professionally, has recorded his experience of reading Leavis as follows: 'I had to read Leavis three times. The first time left me asking "What has he said?" The second time I asked "Is that all?" The third time I said "Now I see." '[11] Different readers would express this quality differently but I think it is a common experience. This experience may under-lie the repeated desire of commentators to give a theoretical account of what he is doing; to isolate analytically the gap between Black's second and third readings; although Leavis himself clearly felt the effect would be to reduce the third again to the second. His style and strategy are such as to resist this.

This quality also underlies some of the difficulty in determining the extent of Leavis's influence as it is a discourse that may well affect readers more than they realise. Apart from the more limited case of avowed discipleship, his presentation of his reading as self-evident has led often enough to its becoming genuinely so for a wide spectrum of readers. His own observation that critics arguing against him seemed on occasion to be depending on his own earlier reading of the work in question, may be amenable to a similar explanation. The nature of his own reading, at least ideally, is indicated by his attitude to its opposite: any activity lending itself to the description 'interpretation'. When he remarks parentheti-cally in this lecture that *The secret sharer* does not 'require the kind of psychological gloss hinted at in the conventional way, by a symposiast in *The London Magazine*' (p. 107), he is claiming the authority not of a rival interpretation but of a principled refusal to overlay the work with meanings of this kind.

I have said that Leavis's way of reading may be 'ideally' defined in the terms I have been outlining, for what has been described here, and earlier with respect to the Yeats lecture, is, if not a self-contradiction, then an accommodation of opposed principles. The ultimate recourse to ostensive assertion underlying even the most minute verbal analysis is more frankly evident in this essay on prose fiction. Yet, as I have said, a purely ostensive procedure is neither possible nor desirable: the critic is there in some way to illuminate the work and guide response. Looked at as a matter of principle, therefore, there is a potential conflict between the collaborative practice enshrined in the phrase 'the common pursuit' and the ostensive self-evidence on which the critical discourse rests. And the appeal to self-evidence is especially dangerous in his case for the existential holism that gives the characteristic force to his criticism means that the moral stakes are high. Misjudgements may occur through failure of attention, but where such a misjudgement is a fully considered one, it is hard to escape the implication of some existential inadequacy in the reader. The lurking conflict between the collaborative and ostensive principles is ironically highlighted by occasions on which Leavis has radically changed his own judgements.

It is striking that in both the Yeats and the Conrad lectures Leavis raises the possibility of his having changed his view of them only to reaffirm the essential rightness of his earlier assessment. But in the major instance of Dickens, on whom he changed his mind so radically between *The great tradition* and *Dickens the novelist*, he notoriously made no reference to his earlier judgement. This can hardly have been through simple forgetfulness since he repeated the same essay on *Hard times* while dropping the crucial sentence referring to the rest of Dicken's *œuvre*. Whether that was disingenuous on his part is harder to say since the reversal was after all performed publicly. What is revealed, perhaps, is the difficulty for him of collaborative disagreement even with his earlier self. A recognition of his own earlier failure to respond adequately to Dickens might well have provided a way into his later understanding for his readers, who presumably require this induction or they would have no need to read the book. And it might have made such a reader's state of mind sympathetically available as a starting-point. But it is as if the holism and self-evidence of the mature reading has effaced the earlier experience. It is a striking instance of the conflict between ostensive self-evidence and collaboration.

But the point of looking at his practice in this principled way is not to propose a disabling contradiction; it is to suggest why his discourse does not lend itself to theoretical extrapolation of that kind. Properly critical discourse as Leavis understood it, that is a discourse concerned with discriminations of value and significance, has to meet these conflicting demands. It is an impersonal, or objectified, account of what can only be personal. I believe that Leavis's rhetoric is peculiarly conscious of an intrinsic conflict rather than confused by an avoidable one. It is possible to minimise or disguise this inherent conflict by appealing to an ideological frame of reference or by assuming consensus in the readership but, even where consensus apparently exists, Leavis wishes precisely to make the implied existential commitments fully conscious. The value of literature for him lies in its capacity to do this.

Perry Anderson has expressed the philosophical incoherence of his practice as 'an insistent metaphysical vocabulary combined with a positivist methodology'.[12] If Leavis were attempting to formulate an overall theory this might be a damaging combination. But Leavis is concerned with the nature of significance in language. The 'metaphysical' and the 'positivist' are rather the ideal poles, neither of them purely attainable, between which significance comes into being in Leavis's creative conception of language. All the critic, or reader, has is the 'words on the page' but what we might understand by that phrase will depend, at the least, on a larger conception of language. I have suggested that Leavis's conception of language as an index of the quality of being, and as the very means by which significances are created and known, questions precisely this polarity. His view of the gestural and enactive significance of language challenges the dualism habitually imposed at the level of meaning. Anderson's discussion ignores this fundamental premiss on which Leavis's practice rests. One may, of course, dissent from Leavis's view of language, or even find it beneath discussion, but it is the ground of his practice and Anderson's ignoring of it is symptomatic and characteristic. I don't think he is leaving it out; it just does not register in his terms at all.

Leavis's own discourse is not an attempt to translate literary works into a philosophical account; indeed he insists that they are usually untranslatable in that respect. His criticism is an attempt to participate in the creative act of the work using a discourse that accepts the creative premisses of imaginative literature. 'Dwelling' within the work, but with his own personality and experience rather than the writer's, he performs a holistic act of mixed endorsement and dissent, an act of discovery bearing on both the self and the work, and which is analogous to the primary creative act of composition. Anderson comments on Leavis's appeal to the word 'life' (in Leavis's approving account of Lawrence's *The daughters of the vicar*) that the meaning of the word is entirely circular; it means only what the tale demonstrates it to mean. But what about Lawrence's use of such a term? Is that illegitimate, or meaningless, because it is only given an ostensive and dramatic definition? Leavis's later insistence that ' "life" is a necessary word' was an insistence that critical discourse must have some way of recognising, if not translating, or theoretically accounting for, the recognitions at stake in works of literature. The act of reading, although it is conditioned by the text concerned, should be as fundamental as the act of creation. The danger with proscribing Leavis's kind of usage is that it may entail proscribing much of our literature; or, more precisely, much of the significance of our literature.

In sum, the openness of Leavis's central terms is a way of pointing up such significances in literary texts without translating them into another, inappropriate discourse. It is an attempt to preserve the integrity of the text while analysing it. The word 'maturity' in the present lecture is 'defined' by participation in the young captain's experience; with this in turn seen as an analogue of Conrad's own. It may be that the theme of the work, and Leavis's admiration for Conrad's achievement at large, lead him in some measure to overvalue this tale, but the standard of maturity that is being invoked seems to me to acquire a clear and appropriate definition. If it means only what the tale itself can justify that is no bad thing. Indeed it is a double point of accuracy: it means neither less nor more than it should.

Perhaps the recognition that should be taken from Leavis's later use of Michael Polanyi and Marjorie Grene lies here. His appeal to these writers' accounts of the personal factors in knowledge, particularly in science, has been seen as a sign of his philosophical naïvety. I think myself that Polanyi's strength is not in epistemology or ontology as self-sufficient areas of enquiry. His shrewdness is of a more pragmatical kind directed at the collaborative processes by which knowledge is acquired and tested. It is rather in their a-philosophical aspects that Polanyi and Grene provide an analogue to Leavis's conception of critical discourse. His concern for emotional quality and moral truth values is no more, and no

less, contingent on a theoretically coherent ontology than that of
the poets and novelists who were his exemplars. He seeks to reflect
the disciplined indeterminacy, the controlled and heuristic suggestiveness, of creative usage; and he does so with a demonstrative
self-awareness.

Tradition

It is apparent from the preceding discussion that the word
'maturity' is closely bound up with the term 'tradition' which
covers in turn the merchant service in the tale; the English
language into which Conrad was adopted; and, we might now
add, the critic's own attempt to use that language in a way that is
properly responsive and responsible. What Leavis means to invoke
by 'tradition' is the fundamental premiss of both his specifically
literary criticism and his overall historical critique. Yet, by the
same token, it is so large and problematic an entity as to elude
summary definition. This word points, therefore, to the heart of
Leavis's endeavour in its most controversial and problematic
aspects. In the light of what has been said concerning the general
premisses of his critical discourse it is worth considering more
closely his use of this word in the specific context invoked by this
lecture.

We might say that 'tradition' stands to 'maturity' as 'impersonality' stands to 'sincerity'. In each case there is a recognition of a
value beyond the self. If sincerity is the achieving of impersonality
then tradition is an important means for doing so. And in each
case a word from the personal moral sphere is defined by another
term of largely literary provenance. 'Tradition' is, therefore,
another term involving the interpenetration of 'literary' and 'non-
literary' usage in a way that is either challenging or confused; it
tries to impart to common usage the significance gained from a
specialised one. In this respect it also exemplifies once again how
Leavis stands at the point of interaction between the modernist
literary generation and the native English line of cultural critique.

The idea of tradition was especially important to the modernist
generation and is central to such masterpieces as *The waste land* and
Ulysses. 'Tradition' took on a special importance because of its felt
absence. The interest in tradition was not backward-looking but
focused on the nature of originality and the creative interaction
of the new and the old. In short, the achievement of modern

literature entailed a fundamental understanding of tradition in its inward and creative dimensions. Leavis shared this general awareness but with his own emphasis. Eliot, Joyce and Pound with their practitioners' concerns and their cosmopolitan provenance focused on what Eliot called 'the mind of Europe'.[13] The specifically modernist end of the spectrum of modern literature may be defined in part by its international outlook.[14] Leavis's concern was with moments of supreme or original achievement as manifestations of, or as enabled by, the nature of the language as a whole. His special focus on the English, and to some extent the American, tradition was because of the distinctive nature of the native tongue; what Conrad called the 'genius of the language'.

Not being himself a creative writer with an individual technique or vision to develop, Leavis concentrated on the language itself as the embodiment of the national tradition. Language for him exemplified very concretely the way in which individual and creative usage arise from the inherited forms. It also provides, in its impersonal capacity as *'langue'*, a body of criteria for judging the individual utterance, or *'parole'*.[15] Individuals may use language speciously, or self-indulgently, but they can also be shown to do so. Our language reveals us. The fact that 'we do not belong to ourselves' is enshrined in the very nature of language. And language retains its impersonal dimension even in the most individual utterances. The great writers are those who, like Blake, have the capacity to experience, indeed to write *for*, this impersonality. Language is so primary and habitual in our understanding and expression that it is almost as elusive as 'tradition'; but not entirely so because it can be concretely instanced without losing its subjective character. We certainly tend to read over language as the always rather arbitrary instrument of thought. And this tendency is to some extent encouraged by the Saussurean revolution. For a technical recognition of the interdependence of language and thought, and a corresponding willingness to attend closely to language, does not necessarily entail Leavis's sense of language as encapsulating qualities of experience; as constituting a mode of being. The kind of ontologically radical recognition in respect of language that Heidegger reached through a philosophical study of Being, Leavis reached through his awareness of language as the embodiment of a national experience; as the medium of tradition.

It is appropriate, therefore, that Leavis should open a lecture involving the particular moral tradition of the master mariner by considering the more subliminal registers of the traditional in

Conrad's adoption by the English language. For there is a significant interplay of consonance and contrast between these two spheres. The young captain has, on the whole, chosen his career while Conrad has been 'chosen' by the language. At the same time each position has strong overtones of the other. The more unconscious workings of tradition are likely, perhaps, to be the most compelling yet Conrad, as an emigré, was able to endorse in consciousness a decision that he felt as a necessity. This mixture of choice and necessity lies at the heart of Leavis's conception of tradition and is the point by which it needs to be compared to opposed conceptions. When Eliot defended the idea of tradition in 'Tradition and the individual talent' his assumed opponent was a view of tradition as an external form imposing its inertia on the individual experience. Hence his emphasis on the inward and dynamic meaning of tradition. By the late twentieth century the common counter-conception has changed. The habitual objection to 'tradition' now is on grounds of 'ideology'. For proponents of the 'hermeneutics of suspicion' the term 'tradition' lends an illegitimately honorific value to a given set of mutually reinforcing assumptions and practices. Rather than an external and inert weight it has become an insidiously internal and dynamic constituent of apparently spontaneous, individual experience. The task of the examined life, to say nothing of a liberating politics, therefore, is to expose and neutralise its workings.

This argument often suffers from a rhetorical Manicheanism which is likely to falsify the very experience it seeks to investigate. It is difficult to concentrate on the exposure of ideological structures without implying that they are *only* mystifying and deceptive and therefore placing oneself outside them sympathetically as well as analytically. But those who live within traditional structures of feeling and practice are not necessarily mystified by them. The value of such structures lies largely in the way they are understood by those who live within them. To weigh the positive value of a given tradition as a resource of past experience against its danger as a mystifying potency it is necessary to be in some measure inward with it and accepting of its premises. Conrad's adoption into English and the captain's assumption of command epitomise this dual understanding from the other side. They are not concerned to deconstruct their respective traditions but the fact of their consciously 'joining' in each case signifies a relative awareness of other possibilities. English was not a 'choice' for Conrad yet clearly another writer might have felt a different need. And it is brought home forcibly to the young captain, when he hears of his predecessor's effective treason and suicide, that the tradition he has joined is precisely an ideal one and not the historical sum of past practice. Tradition is an historical potency, and significance, rather than a set of events. Without the force of tradition, the events would have a different meaning or might not have occurred. And, by the same token, the tradition cannot be analytically understood without a recognition of its experiential weight and irreducibility as a form of commitment. Tradition is intrinsically ideal but not an 'idea'.

If we were seeking to define the proper balance between critical understanding and inward sympathy in any complex experience, one of the most natural examples, perhaps, would be the reading of a work of literature. Here is a complex of value and reference which cannot be reduced to paraphrase or to a single plane of meaning yet which has been purposively constructed and can therefore be apprehended and judged as an overall significance. Hence, for Leavis, a poem is not only part of a tradition, ultimately that of the language itself, it provides the ideal training for combining inwardness with critical understanding. A work of literature may reflect ideological structures naïvely or objectionably but critical reading is the act of understanding this. Another work may illuminate the positive strength of the tradition concerned. In *Pamela* and *The pilgrim's progress*, perhaps, we can see the two kinds of interest. This places a great burden on the critic and provides no general procedural means for carrying it. But rather than appeal to an ideological analysis brought to the work, Leavis sees the work itself as the most significant objectification of the author's creative understanding. A critic is someone able to respond fully to the author's premises without being gulled by them.

I do not wish to endorse all Leavis's specific judgements or his entire historical analysis but it is important to recognise that his ideal of reading engages the problematic nature of tradition and attempts to meet it with an appropriately holistic attention. He engages a real problem for which the triumphant brandishing of half-truths is no solution. His strength and limitation in this respect are that he spoke from *inside* his tradition in the way that Conrad and his young captain were in theirs: not naïvely, but committedly. Like them he had ultimately no way of enforcing this on those who did not share his commitment. In so far as this is a limitation it is an intrinsic rather than an arbitrary one. And to that extent I believe it is peculiarly valuable, if one does not share his commitment, to appreciate the recognitions it uniquely generated rather than use its built-in lack of theoretical universality as a reason for not attending at all. For to be outside the complex of commitments invoked by this particular sense of tradition may be at least equally partial with respect to its value as a mode of life and perhaps much more so. Of course, for Leavis no English speaker *can* be outside the tradition.

These considerations may be brought to bear on the most controversial locus of Leavisian tradition: 'the organic community'. In the light of their reading of English as used over several centuries, and with the social-historical investigations this reading entailed, the Leavises believed that the quality of English as the medium of public and private experience had declined.[16] And this was itself the index of a general change in the culture epitomised perhaps in our very use of the word 'society' rather than 'community'. One of the authors to whom Leavis appealed to exemplify this was George Sturt (George Bourne) whose *Change in the village* (1912) and *The wheelwright's shop* (1923) chronicled the period of his own lifetime during which the ancient trade of the village wheelwright gave way to a motor repair shop. In itself, Sturt's account of this rural trade is impressive. There is the slow acquisition of skill including the knowledge of wood; the making of carts for specific farmers who will use them locally, and bring them for repair, for years to come; and the intrinsic relation of beauty and utility in the product. All this is described in a concrete way and not as an exercise in nostalgia. This was the period in which Sir James Frazer, working on *The golden bough*, was able to exemplify ancient rituals in the rural customs surviving throughout the European countryside. Lawrence's *The rainbow* and Yeats's collections of folk-tales reflect a similar awareness of very ancient forms of life persisting albeit in residual and much modified ways. The Great War, the new mass production phase of industrialism and the commercial exploitation of universal literacy were all factors producing a massive change within, or by, the first two decades of the new century.

Leavis believed that the kind of cultural changes in question here presented problems for the modern world which could not be adequately addressed on the political plane alone; at least not within the range of political conceptions actually available. He was himself a supporter of the Liberal party in so far as he could give his commitments political expression at all. The diminishing sense in which he felt able to do this may be reflected in the larger historical arena by what George Dangerfield has chronicled as *The strange death of Liberal England*. Politics, in Leavis's view, would be the necessary means of implementing any large social understanding that could be achieved but it was not the means of generating that understanding. He therefore looked to the universities to conduct, or to lead, the kind of self-analysis that society required. He believed that the national literature was a crucial resource in this task not just as an historical record but as a training in a holistic mode of understanding. He also believed, along with some of the major modern writers, that there were very important clues for understanding the present and for directing the future in the forms of life which were passing away. The phrase 'organic community' encapsulates the qualities at stake in that respect.

Now the notion of the 'organic community' has attracted more dismissive criticism than any other aspect of Leavis's endeavour and it is, I believe, more problematic than he allowed. At the same time, its precise claims have sometimes been misunderstood, and I should briefly indicate some of the pertinent discriminations. The principal objection is that it is a conservative idyll, a nostalgic projection on to the past, which distorts the true history of rural life. Raymond Williams has pointed out that this belief in the recent decline of rural life is itself a tradition going back through Cobbett to Langland and that rural capitalism has eroded the quality of community life from the middle ages onwards. There never was an organic community except as a potent myth.[17] The counter case is that Leavis was not equating the quality of communal culture with a sum of human felicity. He was not talking about the conditions in which people have had to live so much as the language and the sense of human significances which they had available, and had themselves collectively created, for doing so. To insist on the quality of life as opposed to the standard of living is not to deny the importance of the latter. His critics see him as belittling the sufferings of earlier generations; he would see his critics as belittling the cultural achievement of those generations. From this point of view, even the recurrent belief in a recently lost way of life, as Raymond Williams concedes, is itself a manifestation of the persistent demand for a humanly significant communal order. It is an aspect of the traditional identity rather than evidence against it.

Williams's section on the 'organic community' in *Culture and society* remains the classic critique. This is partly because he sees the force of Leavis's account and is concerned not to dismiss it but to see it in the context of other features of pre-industrial rural life such as penury and exploitation. At the same time he recognises that to broaden the scope in that way is to threaten the historical meaningfulness of this conception. Now in so far as Leavis saw his account as historically summative, Williams's objections seem to me entirely cogent. And there is no doubt that Leavis did see it in that way. When he returned to the issue directly in *Nor shall my sword* it was to restate Sturt's account as an historically complete one.[18] But I think the true bearing of Leavis's perception lies on a different plane that Williams does not engage. When Williams suggests that Leavis should include more cultural elements than the literary in his analysis, he is selling Leavis's position short. He exemplifies once again the persistent misunderstanding of what the 'literary' would encompass for Leavis. Leavis's proposed study of the seventeenth century, for example, would have encompassed all fields of enquiry and achievement. The difference is that he would have considered them as forms of language. He would not have focused exclusively on literature as evidence, but he would have used great literature as the standard of complexity and recognition to be brought to bear on cultural expression at large. The ultimate focus is on language, rather than 'literature' in a limiting sense. Behind actual speech there is the potentiality of language. Leavis was trying to identify critically the quality of '*langue*' in and behind '*parole*'.

It should also be said that in so far as the phrase 'organic community' attempts to define the moral quality of a culture rather than its more quantifiable conditions it can be said to be ideal but it is not necessarily, in the simply negative sense, idealised. On several occasions in *Scrutiny* writers touching on this topic pointed out that it was neither possible nor desirable to return to an earlier form of life. And where the English novel or poetic traditions provide the evidence it is not of a simply idealising kind. Q. D. Leavis, in her introduction to *Silas Marner*, points out the positive aspects of rural life as understood by George Eliot but the work also includes the evils of squirearchy, prejudice and superstition which have done so much of the damage in the tale.[19] Political radicalism is itself part of the tradition. Mrs Gaskell's *North and South* is a classic statement of this theme in that the geographical regions referred to in the title come to stand for the heroine's, Margaret Hale's, maturity and youth as she eventually recognises the inadequacy of her earlier rural parsonage existence. The overcoming of her false idealising of rural life is much of the point of the novel. Of course, it remains a matter for critical discrimination to determine how far any of these writers understood their world and how far their own social idealism helped or hindered them in doing so. But the point at issue here is that in assessing the claims of Leavis's phrase it is necessary to distinguish what would constitute evidence for or against. Leavis appealed to representative uses of language in the past which, over and above their referential value, enshrined *in themselves* the quality of culture he was seeking to affirm. From that point of view, statistical evidence of the flight of the rural poor to the new industrial centres would not in itself refute the claim.

Once again, the problem is one of incommensurability. Williams, within his terms, can *add* these areas of consideration to make a larger equation whereas for Leavis they are different in *kind*. Williams sees the significance of words, and of 'structures of feeling' in language, as open to social-historical explanation. Leavis sees language as the means of creating significances which are not so reducible. The quality of the language is for him an ultimate datum. Hence in *Culture and society*, which is social-historical in its interest, the limitations of the 'organic society' are fairly stated. But if there is something further at stake in Leavis's conception which Williams's terms cannot accommodate, it emerges more clearly in Williams's later study of English pastoralism in *The country and the city*. Here the ground is much more literary and, while Williams's demystification of English pastoral is invaluable in itself, it stands in an essentially corrective relation to canonical appreciation and seems unable to account, in a positive way, for the power of the poetry it discusses.

The corresponding difficulty for Leavis lies in the intrinsic nature of the evidence for his conception. It comes, once again, to placing a considerable burden of significance on language itself; and particularly, in this case, on its representativeness. In his introduction to *The pilgrim's progress*, for example, Leavis speaks of the strength and authority the work draws not from its formal doctrine or moral allegory but from its humour, its psychological shrewdness, and its weight of popular social experience as enshrined in its idiom.[20] Indeed, he opens his account by reference to William York Tindall's *John Bunyan: mechanick preacher* which placed Bunyan within an extensive anonymous tradition of itinerant preachers. Yet Leavis adduces Tindall's study in order to demur at the possible reduction of Bunyan to this common denominator and insists on his special genius whereby the common elements were transformed into an enduring and profound expression of popular sensibility. A problem arises here that encompasses Shakespeare as much as Bunyan. To what extent is genius, or major talent, or even an intelligent individual mind like George Bourne's, summative of its culture and to what extent is it transformative? We can see by the results that such writers have absorbed their culture in a profoundly representative way; they imply the general potentiality to which they have given expression. But it is not clear that the logic of this inference can be reversed. What is shown is precisely a potentiality and, however important and impressive that may be, it does not of itself tell us the nature of more average sensibility; particularly when we consider that such representative writers are often inspired largely by opposition to the prevailing culture. Leavis is himself a representatively English figure, but hardly a reliable index of average cultural quality even in the Cambridge of his day. He was the *potential* Cambridge. Representativeness occurs through a creative, but problematic, dialectic with originality.

And Leavis's more general reading of English literature rather accentuates the problem. His concentration on a highly selective list of important writers and his relative lack of interest in writers who do not meet the most demanding criteria places an especially heavy burden on the representativeness of the major figures. In a way, Q. D. Leavis, who gave a more serious and primary attention to many minor writers, is the more entitled to such a view of the major ones. Her reading was more culturally holistic in seeking to accommodate more of the average experience. Mrs Gaskell, for example, whom she treats positively, falls below the threshold of most serious interest to which F.R.L. largely confined himself. But from another point of view, this difference enables us to see the nature of the Leavisian claim more clearly and likewise the problems it entails.

In sum, Leavis's conception of language as the immediate index of being provides him with a penetrating way of reading the utterances of individuals and, in so far as the language is a common possession, this encompasses the representative significance within the individual expression. But when that becomes the basis for historical extrapolations covering the inner lives of large numbers of anonymous individuals it remains speculative rather than evidential. The 'organic community' seems to me, therefore, not such an empty or purely nostalgic conception as it has sometimes been made out to be, yet it falls short of the historical demonstrability that the Leavises claimed for it. That would require a generalised access to subjectivity which in the nature of things we cannot enjoy. At the same time, the representative historical meaning that can be inferred from individual cases, like Bunyan, is not to be dismissed. Bunyan is a witness to his times both in what he says and in what he is. We should give due weight to both planes of significance. It remains an important, if problematic, comment on his culture that it could have 'produced' him.

In short, we may say that, as with Conrad's captain, the traditional inheritance is a potentiality that can only be realised in the life of the individual. Otherwise it is purely 'ideal'. Yet for the captain, as for Conrad himself, it was a vivid, compelling and enabling potency not reducible to the external conditions in which it was felt or to the sum of its past incarnations. Indeed, it was felt largely as an opposition to, or a transformation of, those conditions. And past inadequacies only emphasise the responsibilities of the present. Leavis had a comparable conception of the potency of the English language in the past as a means of expressing an ideal of wholeness in both individual and communal life. His real focus was on what he saw as the increasing loss of that potentiality. He had no solution, as he often said, to the problem of an adequate communality in the modern world. But he believed that the inward index of past experience embodied in the language and its literature provided uniquely valuable terms for understanding the nature of the problem. When reading poems we commonly distinguish their intrinsic significance as poems over and above their immediately literal and historical reference. Leavis accords to the language as a whole a comparably problematic, but compelling, significance.

The novel as 'dramatic poem'

What I have been eliciting from this discussion of *The shadow line* lecture and the excursus on 'tradition' is the way in which, for Leavis, fundamental significances for living are embodied in works of literature, and in the language at large, so as to be available for demonstration and yet remain elusive of independent definition in philosophical terms or proof in historical terms. In doing so I have indicated strengths and difficulties in such a conception. In the light of that it will now be possible to consider more closely his phrase 'the novel as dramatic poem' as an indication of his conception of fiction and, by extension, of literature at large.

The issue of genre is highlighted through much of the lecture and on first introducing it Leavis defines the essential qualities of narrative fiction in relation to *Typhoon*:

> But the essential point to make about the tale is that it is the work of a great novelist — a writer, that is, whose interest is centred on his human theme, and the point of whose conception depends on the felicity and convincingness with which his individual human actors are made present to us. (p. 98)

This is a squarely mimetic, realist conception of the novel form. It entails no literal-mindedness yet it assumes the immediate translatability of the novelist's terms into those of everyday human relations and moral psychology. But as he attempts his summary statement on the more complex *The shadow line* he appeals to a rather different emphasis; almost a different principle:

> The point I have to make about the significance of the kind of creative work ('dramatic poem' I have called it) we have in *The Shadow Line* is such that it can't be represented by any moral. I have spoken of 'symbolism': I have not meant to suggest that *The Shadow Line* is symbolic in such a way as to admit of a neat and definitive interpretation.
>
> It is a profound work, and complex in its profundity. Conrad himself (if he could be supposed capable of attempting it!) couldn't have provided an adequate summing up of its significance. If one perceives (as one surely must) that it is significant in the way of the greatest art, one knows that taking and pondering the significance must be a matter, first of sensitive response, then of a delicate balancing of one suggestion or intimation against another until the whole, in one's sense of it, has settled into the right inclusive poise. (pp. 108–9)

I have reproduced this passage at some length here as it epitomises much of the rhetoric and procedure just outlined in this lecture and it also rehearses the larger shift in terms already seen in *The great tradition*. It offers a conception of fiction which, appealing to the term 'dramatic poem', attempts to penetrate behind mimesis for 'significance'. He is harking back to E. M. Forster's comment on Conrad's philosophical elusiveness and insisting on the positive value of this quality in Conrad's best work. Undoubtedly he is reflecting the specifically modern aspect of Conrad. Frank Kermode has discussed at length in *The romantic image* the preoccupation in modern literature and criticism with the integral image; an image that so subsumes its meaning as to be significant but untranslatable. We think of this primarily in connection with poetry but not exclusively. And it is noteworthy in this respect that Leavis developed the formula 'dramatic poem' especially for learning to read the first truly modern novels of D. H. Lawrence: *The rainbow* and *Women in love*. Some commentators, as I have noted, see a distinct difference between the mimetic assumptions governing *The great tradition* and the 'poetic' model used for Leavis's discussion of modern fiction. I am inclined to emphasise the aspect of continuity. For the controlled indeterminacy of the fiction, its exploratory openness, uses mimesis as its necessary, and testing, vehicle. The composition of the work was an act of discovery, a use of the known to engage the unknown, and this, as has been suggested, has deep roots in the history of English fiction.

It is revealing in this connection that P. N. Furbank, reviewing Conrad's letters with their agonising record of 'writer's block', quotes *The shadow line* as an intimation of what this experience meant to Conrad.[21] The frustration of the becalmed ship, the darkness and the penetration into the unknown are, Furbank argues, an effective image of how, for Conrad, the frustrating blankness of the writer's block was not an extrinsic agony preventing him from writing: it was the very source, the necessary absence of preconception, from which his greatest creative discoveries were won. That gives a more specific expressive weight to the sense of creative struggle *through* narrative and character which animates Leavis's reading of this tale and of fiction at large. In coming to terms with prose fiction as a genre worthy of the most serious attention, Leavis was not importing in an external way the category of the poetic. He was finding in prose fiction, seeing it as it were from the standpoint of the author, an equivalent for the enactive, heuristic value that was more immediately evident in poetry. Mimetic reference to the world is subsumed into that inner dimension of mimesis encapsulated in the enactive conception of language.

In this respect the phrase, with its superimposition of genres, explains the peculiarly intense perception of quality and the corresponding restriction of range in Leavis's reading of fiction. We might say that whereas Dr Johnson tended to read poetry as if it were prose, Leavis read prose fiction as if it were poetry. And this has an implication for poetry too. For if the novel can be seen as essentially a kind of poem, then by the same token a poem may be considered as a kind of novel. In this sense the phrase indicates the characteristic Leavisian territory in both genres; or, we might say, in literature at large. *The great tradition*, rather than shifting from the 'mimetic' to the 'expressive', moves between the necessary poles of literary significance.

To explore this proposition we should avoid having too literal and external an understanding of these generic terms which are often used as analytic tools over the head of their immediate technical meaning. Hence Joyce's use of 'lyric', 'epic' and 'dramatic' referred to qualities which could be present or missing in lyric verse, prose fiction or theatre respectively. And it is notable that just as Joyce, a novelist, defined his ideal of impersonality as 'dramatic' so Brecht, a dramatist, defined his comparable ideal of impersonality as 'epic' (i.e. narrative) theatre. Leavis's use of the terms 'novelist' and 'poetic' in these passages has a similar doubleness of reference to a formal genre and an artistic quality. Taken in this qualitative rather than technical sense 'novel' and 'poem' suggest the constant poles of possibility between which, for Leavis, literary significance is created.

As I indicated in discussing Leavis's view of language, his sense of significance is by no means literalistic. The creative possibility in language depends on its being a symbolic medium and this exploratory potentiality is what he means in this context by the 'poetic'. At the same time, as indicated in the discussion of Yeats, he is not prepared to extend this realm of the symbolic to encompass a speculative, or aesthetic, domain in which human values would have to be held in abeyance. The meaningfulness of the symbolic action lies in its being a means of exploring, and by implication affirming, the value of living. Hence the symbiotic structure of his critical rhetoric which reflects the symbiosis of language and experience from which significance arises. This tangible reference to the experiential is encapsulated in the term 'novel'. His overall view of literature is a combination of the poetic and the novelistic in these mutually qualifying senses. The exploratory openness and the experiential concreteness take on their significance in relation to each other. 'Novel' and 'poem' are the poles between which meaning is generated. Leavis's favoured novelists and poets are those who lend themselves to this creative use of a symbolic mimesis: responsive and moral life enacted in language.

In his hands this is a powerful and dynamically inward way of reading but its peculiar penetration entails some serious exclusions as the spectrum of possibilities within each of these genres extends away from this area of overlap. Hence the imposition of authorial will in Fielding, Sterne or Joyce prevents the kind of heuristic, enactive use of language, or mimesis, that Leavis takes as the locus of significance. They all, of course, play with the mimetic possibilities of language but precisely their self-consciousness in doing so inhibits that sense of writing for, and learning from, the language that Leavis identified in Blake or Lawrence. And similarly, in respect of poetry, the 'musical' principle running through Spenser and Tennyson commited the language to a mode which could not, except intermittently, realise the enactive potentiality by which the experience, in Leavis's conception, was testable.

This is another way of defining the narrowness often objected to in his judgements. All worthwhile critics have their special domains within which they can respond more illuminatingly. But the peculiarity of Leavis is the way in which literature falling outside of his area of concern was not just a matter of intelligent interest or even indifference but was an active affront to his sense of quality. I hope it is evident from what has been said that this is not an arbitrary or temperamental limitation. It arises from the fundamental logic of his understanding of creative responsibility. And the issue of narrowness is worth considering further in the light of other aspects already touched on in this study.

W. A. Hart has acutely pointed out that Leavis's generalised dismissal of 'philosophy' as an aid to literary critical understanding and even his later, equally generalised, remarks on its useful 'co-presence' with the study of literature, both suffer from a lack of internal discrimination about philosophy which arises from not taking it seriously enough.[22] Leavis accepted the activities of certain academic philosophers as representing the whole possibilities of philosophy; a mistake he would not dream of making with respect to literary criticism. And when in his later years he drew support from the writings of Michael Polanyi and Marjorie Grene he specifically denied taking a philosophical interest in them. As I have remarked at an earlier point, he may have been essentially right in that but again it is not a distinction which, as Hart observes, he would have allowed in respect of a literary work. Only when the work has been understood in its own terms can it be adduced, or 'used' in other contexts. The point Hart makes in regard to philosophy can be extended into the literary domain too.

I have suggested that in making his large diagnostic critique of Milton's language Leavis gestures towards a more discriminated, comprehensive response which he does not actually spell out. This happens in varying degrees with many authors about whom he has made general statements of a comparably diagnostic kind. Certainly Fielding, Sterne and Joyce are writers of enormous intrinsic as well as historical interest. For what it is worth, I have myself written positively on all three of them in other contexts. Yet I believe Leavis's fundamental, or as I have called it his diagnostic, assessment of them is essentially right. He is concerned with the fundamental premisses of their uses of language and their corresponding grip on experience. We have to consider, however, what is done within these premisses and each of these three do remarkable and experientially illuminating things within theirs. It is as if, having decided what the creative premisses of a given author are, Leavis is fully attentive to the complexity of discrimination which his favoured authors, such as Lawrence, require but is unable to contemplate comparably complicating factors in others; or indeed to grant any possible value being created within their premisses. But surely much of the business of criticism lies precisely here.

The novelist who most strikingly focuses the general point here is Proust; and once again it is indicative that he is not from the English tradition. There are ways of accommodating most British writers to Leavis's conception even if it is not the most productive way of reading some of them. In Proust, however, there is a direct challenge. Proust presents a highly considered and coherent vision which from its own point of view is comprehensive. The point of view hardly meets the criterion of 'maturity' in an everyday sense. It explicitly rests on an emotional arrestation and uses as its principal vehicles a predatory homosexual, a courtesan and a lesbian; three figures who, in the given social culture and narrative circumstances, lend a particular cast to Proust's analysis of illusion as a constitutive element in human emotion: the only true paradise is the paradise lost. But Proust is one of those writers who use the idiosyncratic instance as a denaturalising point of leverage for a fresh understanding of the universal. His study of love, imagination and art is a classic vision. He represents a whole truth, subtly and impersonally, as seen from its particular standpoint; the recognition of the standpoint being, of course, an element of its comprehensiveness. In short, we are faced with the indubitable maturity of Proust *as artist*.

Such a distinction between man and artist is not one that Leavis can accommodate. It is quite different from the unease we might feel in comparing Tolstoy's works with what we know of his life. Tolstoy's greatest works, we could argue, are those in which he transcended his personal limitations and obsessions. In so far as it is shocking to realise aspects of his character as a man this only highlights the creative function of his art as Leavis would define it. But in Proust's case the 'unacceptable' element is placed at the heart of the work. It is not just part of the creative struggle, something to be overcome: it is one of the predicates of the finished work. In prose fiction, Proust provides a test case comparable to Milton in poetry: a major writer whose personal nature Leavis can shrewdly assess but whose artistic achievement he therefore cannot 'recognise'.

I place the word 'recognise' here in quotation marks because it is ambiguous. It may be taken in its diplomatic sense of acknowledging legitimacy. In so far as Leavis wishes to give priority to the most fundamental orders of significance, and is writing for a world bedevilled by inert relativism and conventionality, this non-recognition may be understood tactically. But in the light of his understanding of creative significance there is clearly something more intrinsic at stake. He is rather unable within his terms to understand or see literary possibilities which do not reflect that struggle towards a normative self-realisation on which the best of Conrad, Lawrence or Tolstoy depend. And to the extent that this intrinsic implication of 'recognise' pertains it undermines the value of a tactical one. It leaves much of our literature in a kind of limbo. Taking this in conjunction with W. A. Hart's comments on Leavis's attitude to philosophy, we might say that his diagnostic suspicion extends to the whole realm of the speculative. This includes not only philosophy but any literary mode in which a bracketing of our existential values is crucial: literature in which the underlying spirit is, in that sense 'philosophical'. Many of us find the distinction between man and artist as enforced by such a case as Proust difficult to accommodate but we feel obliged to live with it. To find *no* difficulty in it is hardly a good symptom, however, and the merit of Leavis's radical position is to highlight the problematic nature of 'literary' significance and to check the

temptation to merely vulgar relativism or vacuous connoisseurship.

In this connection it is worth considering the third term of
Leavis's formula: the word 'dramatic'. This word, like the other
two terms already discussed, has clearly to be taken in a qualitative, rather than a literally generic, sense. In this usage it has
been a crucial term in modern Anglo-American criticism of fiction
and stems particularly from the prefaces and criticism of Henry
James. It denotes the element of experiential specificity on which
the authority of the fictional vision rests. John Killham has criti-
cised the shifting Leavisian use of the related term 'concrete'
which, within the space of a single essay, refers sometimes to the
imaginative creation and sometimes to the extra-literary reality.[23]
Killham is right to remark on this but not perhaps to object. The
Jamesian phrase 'felt life' covers both elements: the external world
and the responsive principle. As I have sought to show, Leavis's
rhetorical practice was to use words frankly as ostensive counters
in which individual momentary use is not intended as the basis
from which a coherent system could be extrapolated. More to the
point, perhaps, the effect of concreteness, or dramatic presentness,
is a spark of significance that flashes *between* separate elements. Art
and life are precisely not one realm or the spark of significance
could not occur. Leavis's rhetoric tries to catch the nature of
reading as this dynamic experience of significance and he therefore
focuses at different moments on its different poles. It cannot be
dealt with literalistically any more than Pope's play on verbal
sounds to reflect on their sense.

But if we accept this enactive conception of mimesis implied in
the word 'dramatic' we may note that it is used not only over the
head of any literal reference to theatre but indeed in frequent
contradistinction to such a possibility. In the Jamesian context the
word refers to elements of enacted self-consciousness and narrative
amplification which could not be rendered on stage. These provide
the significant medium for the literal dialogue which might well
seem thin or precious if extracted and spoken for an audience.
That is not a criticism of James, of course, it is merely to indicate
the nature of his particular achievement as a novelist. But in
respect of the critic we may lean a little harder on this effective
contradistinction between the 'dramatic' and the literally
theatrical which seems to me to have an indicative value for
Leavis's criticism generally.

The intensity of experience 'enacted' in the symbolic mode of language according to Leavis's conception seems to have as its corollary a relative indifference to the values of theatre proper. It may even be indicative that in the above quotation on *Typhoon* Leavis's phrase 'individual human actors' should assimilate a theatrical image so completely to the internal, creative action of the author on the material. More substantively, several commentators, including sympathetic ones, have noted Leavis's relative weakness in dealing with Shakespeare as compared to later English poetry and the novel.[24] His account of *Othello*, for example, seems to miss much of the tragedy.[25] We might agree with him that *Othello* is something more of a domestic 'case' than the other great tragedies, but he reads it in effect as a 'dramatic poem'. That is to say, in his terms, he reads it as a species of novel and, despite his opposition to Bradleyan reading, with a corresponding concentration on character.[26]

The peculiar poignancy of theatre, which great dramatists often exploit formally and thematically, lies in the inescapable, moment-by-moment juxtaposition of real actors and imaginary characters. Theatre of its nature enforces a recognition of the aesthetic use of illusion. The literal stage encompasses a speculative space. Now there is no logical reason for Leavis's general conception not to embrace this area. The cast and director are indeed participating inwardly in the implied creative process of the author; they are seeking the ideal reading that Leavis places at the notional centre of the critical act. And we should remember that the 1920s and 1930, Leavis's formative years as a critic, were not a high point in British theatre or theatrical criticism. But even so it is as if the frankly aesthetic constitution of theatrical experience aroused that suspicion with which he viewed the aesthetic domain at large. His own reading of poetry aloud, like his lecturing style, was enactive but far from histrionic.

Hence, the formula 'novel as dramatic poem', when all the terms are understood in their Leavisian implications, defines his area of peculiar insight and its corresponding limitations. He is an acute, I would say a profound, critic of the existential postures enacted in characteristic uses of language. But his intentness on this diagnostic focus makes him unable to consider occasions on which the language is to be understood in a more relative and speculative way. Part of the strength of this position is that the creative complexities within a work may indeed remain outweighed by the inadequacy of its existential and stylistic premises. *Howards End*, for example, seems to me such a case. And even in those instances in which one sees further qualifications to be made in the author's favour, Leavis's diagnostic judgement is always clear and never trivial so that it is usually pertinent, albeit in a modified way, to the business of reading the work. It is the same authority that characterises D. H. Lawrence's *Studies in classic American literature* in which we may wish to qualify his reading by noting a self-irony in Benjamin Franklin or the narrative obliquity in Poe, and yet Lawrence's essential critique, and his understanding of these writers as part of a larger American character, retains its force. Lawrence has gone for the most fundamental kinds of significance in these writers. In criticism it is not just the 'rightness' of judgements that matters but their order of significance. The influence and importance of Leavis stem from his capacity, even when his specific judgements seem inadequate, to quicken our perception of the order of significance in which literature is to be read.

7

Conclusion

I have sought to examine the rhetorical form of Leavis's literary criticism in its function as an existential critique. In so far as literature is a creative and exploratory enactment of irreducible significances and values, what is at stake for him in the work cannot be expressed in terms more fundamental than those of the work itself, and hence the ostensive procedure which lies, quite consciously, at the heart of his practice. But the 'object' to be displayed is not, as it were, the 'text' on the page so much as the participatory act of reading it. Reading has an analogical relation to the act of composition in that it is a re-creation. Reading depends on the reader and is more comparable to musical performance than it is to musical connoisseurship. By a demonstrative reading Leavis tries to define the quality of being for which the language of the text is the irreducible index. And his belief that poetic language is not merely the instrument for expressing something but is in some sense the very being that is in question, leads him to resist any tendency in his own discourse to become an independent, potentially rival, structure of ideas. Instead he leans on the resources of the common tongue to reflect the struggle of the artist towards new significance. Hence my suggestion that the appropriate terms for appreciating him may be drawn from the poets and novelists who were his exemplars in the use of language. The point is particularly explicit in the following comment arising from his discussion of a line from Eliot's *Burnt Norton*.

> This last clause — in fact the whole sentence — would look odd if examined with analytic rigour. But to say that nevertheless it is justified, some such use of language being

compelled by the effort to initiate intelligent commentary on the text, is to pay tribute to Eliot's creative resource in making language serve him in a basic exploration of experience.[1]

Although far from identifying with Eliot, Leavis seeks a critical discourse which will fit, and reflect, the original.

It remains now to assess the most permanent and living aspects of his work. There are obvious senses in which he is an influential critic. Many of his studies of individual poets and novelists remain critical classics useful both for students taking their first bearings and for mature readers wishing to take stock. His concentration on summative critical judgement provides at the least a clear benchmark for any reader. And hence his impact on the commonly accepted mapping of English literature; an impact which affects even those readers who disagree with him. But if his example has a truly continuing pertinence this must rest on the more fundamental question of his general critical stance and the cogency of his historical critique. Borrowing Isaiah Berlin's distinction between the mental types of the 'hedgehog' and the 'fox', we might say that Leavis is the classic instance of the hedgehog. He knew not a lot of different things, like the fox, but one big thing, and that thing he really knew. A decision about Leavis should, therefore, be a decision about this big thing and not just a piecemeal questioning of specific issues.

Taking his endeavour as a whole, I have already suggested that his essay on Dr Johnson may be a pertinent model for considering his own case. He argues that Johnson, as a critic, is a 'living' classic rather than a figure of historical interest such as, he suggests, Dryden is when considered in the same capacity. Johnson's neo-classical training is the means by which he brings a weight of personal experience to bear on the reading of literature. Johnson had a serious and totally considered view of literature and its place in life. And by the same token, the evident limitations of his conception as we now look back on it are not damaging precisely because they *are* so evident. They have become, as it were, part of its meaning; the necessary concomitant of its particular angle of vision. Hence Leavis insists that its limitations are the condition of its peculiar force. You cannot have the one without the other. Much of this can be applied to Leavis himself. The peculiar intensity of his reading is an intensity of focused experience and is conditional upon his 'narrowness' of range. And, like Johnson's, his frame of reference is that of a particular historical moment. The combination of cultural urgency and existential irreducibility that he brings to the reading of literature, and especially of modern literature, is a defining quality of the modern movement itself. In some measure, then, one can see him in a particular literary historical context and recognise his cogency within those terms.

But comparison of Leavis's own case with his remarks on Johnson indicates difference as well as similarity. That is partly because we see him from an historically less distanced vantage-point. But there is a more intrinsic difference which is signalled by Leavis's reference to Johnson's classical 'training'. In this context the word indicates an order or method that can be in large measure externalised independently of the individual. And, indeed, the positive, if somewhat ironic, value of this robust conception was that Johnson himself could recognise its limitations. He did so in his appeal from 'criticism' to 'experience' in respect of Shakespeare and in his recognition that his actual response to Milton could not be accommodated within his formal principles. But Leavis's conception, with its emphasis on the irreducibility of values and the holism of response, could not admit of such detachment either at the level of principle or at the level of personal taste. He has no Johnsonian inkling of something beyond his terms.

That points to a different way of considering his present significance. I think we have to take him as one possessed of, if not by, a particular vision of the fully realised and examined human life on both the individual and the communal planes. This is an original vision. It is not original in the sense that it has no antecedents for, indeed, a strong sense of tradition is one of its constitutive features. But it is original in the sense that it is primordially grounded. It bears on the philosophical and historical realms but does not draw its premises from them. It is the source from which significances for these realms (questions, aspirations, judgements) are generated. His criticism does not just say that the work 'is so, isn't it?' but that this is the proper demand to make on the work. It offers a weight of considered experience and is therefore open to analysis and disagreement but it is not grounded in, or therefore essentially vulnerable to, argument based on general principle. Part of the reason for its primordiality is that it is not just a conception of criticism, or even of literature, but of the human mode of being in language. And for the same reason it is elusive of proof or of conclusive demonstration. As with Heidegger's view of language, you could decide not to accept it, and you could explain why, but that is not a matter of 'proving' it to be wrong. It would be an existential choice. At one level, the compelling analogy here is our response to a poem. We will respond to it critically in the light of our experience but we would recognise as absurdly jejune an attempt to 'prove' a poem 'wrong'. The distinction matters in that we are more prepared to recognise in respect of poems that the weight of considered experience is not measurable by its philosophical premisses. Chaucer's achievement is not diminished because its late mediaeval cosmology is out-moded. But to put the matter in that way is to express it too negatively and relatively. For the weight of experience as implicitly appealed to in Leavis has a unique and strategic importance.

I have stressed throughout this study Leavis's understanding of language as the basis of his whole endeavour. In doing so I have suggested that historical extrapolations from this response to language, as well as some of the literary judgements based on it, are open to other orders of question. Hence the objections which have been made to him in the light of other literary or social historical viewpoints. But the objections voiced at these levels tend to remain silent with respect to the crucial issue of language itself. The fundamental point, and the area in which Leavis *is* a powerful analyst, tends to be passed over as unproblematic or as if it were not there. The schizophrenic quality of Perry Anderson's account, whereby Leavis is a forceful critic yet intellectually trivial, is only an extreme case of the general difficulty that arises when his real area of strength is not engaged. It is this silence that needs interpreting.

Leavis's concern for language as the collective creation of its speech community has become steadily more *passé*. In a comparatively recent 'state of the art' review of language and knowledge, entitled *The post-modern condition: a review of knowledge*,[2] Jean François Lyotard has discussed the multiplicity of 'languages' into which our culture has irrevocably divided. Part of the post-modern condition is the recognition that there is no 'meta-language'. That is to say, no one language in which all the others are contained and their relativity thereby understood. Now by 'languages' here he means the variety of specialised discourses including those of mathematics and computers. In his account, Lyotard does not even consider 'natural' languages, such as French and English, as contenders for this function. As I have noted, Leavis insisted on the misleading nature of the metaphor whereby such specialised discourses are spoken of as 'languages'. French is a language because it is fully independent of the late Latin from which it developed. French speakers do not need to eke out their expression by recourse to Latin. But the specialised discourses to which Lyotard refers are not languages in that sense. They could not exist for their users independently of a 'natural' speech community. Lyotard offers his account as representative, which it doubtless is in respect of the intellectual arena he has in mind. But from a Leavisian point of view, his account is profoundly unrepresentative because it arises from having got 'language in the head' in something like the sense that Lawrence diagnosed 'sex in the head'. It is a limiting self-consciousness which puts you out of touch with the very experience that is ostensibly in question. One of the paradoxes of language is that we can use it to deny it. This may be an aspect of Wittgenstein's insight noted earlier: 'It is what human beings *say* that is true or false; and they agree in the *language* they use. That is not agreement in opinion but in form of life.' I do not deny the real issues Lyotard means to address and there is undoubtedly more to be said on both sides. But I see little evidence that the essential recognitions at stake in Leavis's understanding of language have been met or assimilated. If he is essentially right about language then a sea-change comes over such an enquiry as Lyotard's. I cannot recall that any objector to Leavis has ever tackled him on that crucial ground and much habitual practice implicitly concedes it.

If Leavis's view of language gives him an especially strategic importance in that general arena, there is a second feature of his vision which helps explain his special impact in the literary critical sphere. T.S. Eliot's caveat concerning critics who use their reading of literary works as vehicles for their own conceptions is as pertinent to modern critical systems as it was to the belle-lettrism he primarily had in mind. But in Leavis's case, even apart from his native gift as a responsive reader, we may note that the intrinsic logic of his vision makes him rather different in this regard. The commitment to a creative and impersonal attending to language is at the heart of his conception. And literature is language used so as to most command that attention. Hence, in so far as there is a personal moral vision seeking expression in his literary criticism, it can only, by its own logic, do so to the extent that it puts itself most genuinely at the disposal of the works. The creative impersonality of the artist has to be met by a corresponding capacity in the reader. Personality is realised in impersonality. As I have suggested earlier this central recognition has implications for the reading, as well as the composing, of creative literature. The peculiar quality of Leavis's best criticism is that it is animated, and therefore animates the work being read, with a charge of significance which is his own and yet which can only be manifest within the work's terms. His capacity to give himself to the work resists abstract definition but it is the enacted test of his whole conception.

Leavis, then, is essentially a prophet and one whose vision is expressed, not adventitiously but essentially, through the medium of literature. To see him as a professional critic whose work is irrelevantly shot through with a personal moralism is to keep the bathwater and lose the baby. You have something useful but have missed its real significance. Prophets are notoriously not recognised close to home. The recognition I am arguing for here is not that of complete agreement or discipleship but simply a recognition of his generic nature. It is only on that basis that he can be properly heard and a community whose public discourse is such that he cannot have a serious hearing is fundamentally impoverished.

Indeed it seems to me that Leavis has something of incalculable importance to say for which we have no comparable spokesman. Partial parallels, such as Heidegger, reflect ultimately on his uniqueness rather than his similarity. It would have been possible to conduct the present exposition, at least in its positive aspects, using simply Leavis's own statements and terms. One reason for not doing so is that, while Leavis could hardly be matched as a polemical expositor of his own convictions, it is notorious that these have repeatedly failed to convince a substantial body of readers; including especially those who invoke 'philosophical' or 'theoretical' criteria. For example, in his last major volume, *The living principle*, Leavis reprinted a series of exemplary readings of short texts with a long introductory chapter on the nature of creative thought from which I have taken the passages considered in a previous chapter. David Pole, a philosopher, had offered a critique of some of the earlier material; a critique which ultimately confirms Leavis's essential point about the trained incapacity to understand. Pole, for example, reduces Leavis's sense of value in literature to a notion of moral improvement in the reader. Pole could only see in what Leavis had said a neo-Benthamite proposition.[3] Hence the artificial critical conundrum with which he ends his essay.[4]

The 'thought' of Leavis seems to have something of that invisibility noted earlier in the artistry of George Eliot and Dickens.

Pole's reading corresponds roughly to Michael Black's second reading, 'Is that all?' Hence my attempt to isolate some of the planes of principle gathered into Leavis's practice is not offered as a substitute for, still less as an improvement on, his own account. It seeks only to meet the apparent difficulties of his practice, as well as the real ones, and direct attention to the condensed implicitness of his thinking. The introductory chapter to *The living principle* summarises the issues raised in this study and my purpose is served if the reader can proceed to Leavis's own exposition, not necessarily with complete agreement, but with a proper attention. In particular, by using Heidegger to focus the nature of that attention, I have not meant to suggest that Leavis needs Heidegger. It is rather Leavis's readers who have, in many cases, shown such a need. Indeed, Leavis, in many ways, underwrites Heidegger rather than the reverse; particularly when it comes to an understanding of what it means to speak a common tongue. But mention of a 'common tongue' introduces my final emphasis: there is a reverse side to the coin of uniqueness.

The tendency of the preceding remarks has been to highlight the distinctiveness of Leavis although with the implicit recognition that the personal may also be the representative. And at the opening of this study I noted that the importance of Leavis lies partly in his being a peculiarly representative instance of the act of reading. Hence it may well have struck the reader that many of the qualities I have drawn attention to in Leavis's critical discourse are to be found in much, perhaps any, good, critical writing. This has been a conscious feature of my exposition because it is a conscious aspect of Leavis's criticism to offer a demonstrative definition of reading. We are now perhaps in a better position to appreciate the force of this.

Because Leavis wrote with a prophetic purpose he made the existential commitments of his reading especially salient. Antaeus-like, he maintains a 'grounded judgement'. But all criticism, or any reading which responds to literature at a level beyond the pastime, involves existential commitments. I remarked at an earlier point that an important positive impetus in criticism over the last two decades has come from the resurgence of feminism which, I suggested, has been significantly enabled by broadly Marxian modes of critique. Yet it is presumably not controversial to note that the ideological plane of feminism has also given licence to, and actually occasioned, arguments both self-regarding and self-fulfilling.[5] In other words, the enabling value of such an ideological

136

critique still requires the authority of experience contingent on an impersonal responsibility in the individual. There is always a danger of not knowing what the more implicit, but indispensable, premisses of critical activity are. This sense of responsibility governs Leavis's criticism at all times and he can therefore illuminate the implicit, but often unacknowledged, processes of judgement. These equally underlie theoretically self-conscious practices which seek either to eschew them or simply to take them for granted as if they were automatically guaranteed by the ideological stance. Henry James said of criticism that there is no answer but to be very 'intelligent'. Lawrence said the critic can only record the 'sincere emotion' occasioned by the work. Such formulations are unhelpfully truistic and it is understandable that we should wish to give a more principled elaboration of the critical craft. But not perhaps if it makes us lose touch with these truisms as if there were some kind of alternative to them. To meditate on the truth of the truistic is also necessary. What has been said concerning 'thinking' and 'sincerity' in this account of Leavis will indicate how James and Lawrence, in their characteristic ways, are saying the same thing. It seems to me to be an important, if elusive, thing and part of Leavis's value is to make accessible the truth within the truism.

Much of the day-to-day activity of literary criticism rests implicitly on the kind of premisses concerning language and significance outlined in this study. The difference between Leavis and many academic practitioners is not one of principle but of seriousness. It sometimes appears to be one of principle because Leavis's phenomenology of reading focuses on the subliminal, or tacit, dimension of language. For any student of literature, or language, who wishes to arrive at an understanding of the nature of 'literary' significance, Leavis surely remains an indispensable figure to come to terms with. Provided, of course, that this is based on a holistic appreciation of his stance and not on a set of isolable principles. For Leavis focuses the inescapable responsibility of criticism. Indeed, his concentration is so unswervingly on the heart of the matter in this respect that he has only the narrowest path to tread at times between the ineffable and the banal. He is then like a man staring into the sun. Faced so directly, the source of illumination is blinding. But this directness is also his preeminent importance. He is a uniquely challenging example of what responsiveness to life in language might mean.

Notes

Leavis's principal publications are cited by title and page numbers only; other details are given in the Chronological List on page 147.

Editor's Foreword

1. See for instance Francis Mulhern, *The moment of 'Scrutiny'* (New Left Books, London, 1979).

2. F. R. Leavis, 'Literary criticism and philosophy: a reply', *Scrutiny*, *VI*, 1 (1937), 59–70.

3. See F. R. Leavis, *The living principle: 'English' as a discipline of thought* (Chatto & Windus, London, 1975).

4. See Tom Nairn, 'The English literary intelligentsia', in *Bananas*, ed. Emma Tennant (Blond & Briggs, London, 1977), pp. 57–83; also Perry Anderson, 'Components of the national culture', *New Left Review*, *50* (May/June 1968), 3–57.

5. T. S. Eliot, *Notes towards the definition of culture* (Faber & Faber, London, 1948).

6. Nairn, op. cit., p. 77.

7. See especially T. S. Eliot, 'Tradition and the individual talent' and 'The metaphysical poets', in *Selected essays* (Faber & Faber, London, 1964), pp. 3–11 and 241–50.

8. See Leavis, 'Milton's verse', in *Revaluation: tradition and development in English poetry* (Chatto & Windus, London, 1936).

9. See the chapter on Shelley in *Revaluation*.

10. For a number of de Man's late essays on this topic, see his posthumous volume *The resistance to theory* (University of Minnesota Press, Minneapolis, 1986).

11. See the essay on Keats in *Revaluation*.

12. Three of these essays — 'Thought and emotional quality', 'Imagery and movement' and 'Reality and sincerity' — are reprinted in Leavis, *The living principle*.

13. Paul de Man, 'The return to philology', in *The resistance to theory*, pp. 21–6; p. 25.

14. Ibid., p. 25.

15. Ibid., p. 25.

16. This review ('William Empson: intelligence and sensibility') is reprinted in Leavis, *'Revaluation in criticism' and other essays* (Cambridge University Press, Cambridge, 1986), pp. 2–8.

17. Leavis, 'Joyce and the "Revolution of the word"', *Scrutiny*, *II* (1933), 193–201.

18. De Man, 'The return to philology', p. 24.

19. De Man, 'The resistance to theory', in *The resistance to theory*, pp. 3–20; p. 11.
: 20. See especially Harold Bloom's sequence of books, from *The visionary company* (Doubleday, New York, 1961) to *Wallace Stevens: the poems of our climate* (Cornell University Press, Ithaca, NY, 1977).
21. See Hartman, Bloom, Miller *et al.*, *Deconstruction and criticism* (Seabury Press, New York, 1979).

Chapter 1

1. A notable exception is John Casey's principled defence of Leavis in *The language of criticism* (Methuen, London, 1966), pp. 153–78. Yet this is a theoretical endorsement of Leavis's practice not concerned with the critical cogency of his judgements.

Chapter 2

1. 'Sketch for an English School', *Scrutiny, IX* (1940), 2, 98–120.

Chapter 3

1. Cf. Wellek's 'Literary criticism and philosophy', *Scrutiny, V* (1937), 4, 375–83. Leavis's 'Literary criticism and philosophy: a reply', *Scrutiny, VI*, 1, 59–70 is reprinted in *The common pursuit*.
2. *New Left Review, 50* (1968), esp. 49–56.
3. Fred Inglis, *Radical earnestness* (Martin Robertson, Oxford, 1982), pp. 91–108.
4. 'Arnold as critic', *Scrutiny, VII* (1938), 3, 319–32; 'Coleridge in criticism', *Scrutiny, IX*, (1940), 1, 57–69; 'Johnson as critic', *Scrutiny, XII* (1944), 3, 187–204; 'T. S. Eliot as critic', *Commentary*, Nov. 1958. The Johnson and Eliot essays are reprinted in *'Anna Karenina' and other essays*.
5. 'In memory of Henry James', *Egoist, V* (1918), 1–2.
6. *Twilight of the idols*, 'Skirmishes of an untimely man', section 5.
7. Leavis attacked the reduction of culture to economics in 'Under which king, Bezonian?', *Scrutiny, I* (1932), 3, 205–14. Replies by Morton and Butterfield appeared as 'Culture and leisure' and 'History and the Marxian method' in *Scrutiny, I* (1933), 4. Leavis's next full statement on the 'social history' theme is 'Literature and society', *Scrutiny, XII* (1944), 1, 2–11. 'Bezonian' is reprinted in *Determinations* and 'Literature and society' in *The common pursuit*.
8. This is a principal theme of *William Morris: romantic to revolutionary* (Merton Press, London, 1955).
9. 'Coleridge in criticism', 69.

10. Ibid., 66–8.

11. Reprinted in *The world we imagine* (Chatto & Windus, London, 1969), pp. 3–23.

12. Cf. principally *Of grammatology*, trans. Gayatri Chakravorty Spivak (Johns Hopkins University Press, Baltimore Md, 1976); *Writing and difference*, trans. Alan Bass (Routledge & Kegan Paul, London, 1978).

Chapter 4

1. Ferdinand de Saussure, whose principal work was *Cours de linguistique générale* (Geneva, 1916).

2. 'Memories of Wittgenstein', *The Human World*, no. 10 (Feb. 1973).

3. *Philosophical investigations*, trans. G. E. Anscombe (Blackwell, Oxford, repr. 1968), p. 8.

4. Leavis was very clear about the general impact of Wittgenstein in *The living principle*, p. 13.

5. For example, Fred Inglis, *Radical earnestness* (Martin Robertson, Oxford, 1982), p. 102 and Bernard Sharratt, *Reading relations* (Harvester Press, Brighton, 1982), p. 146.

6. The collections of essays mentioned in this chapter are *What is called thinking?* trans. F. P. Wieck and J. Glenn Gray (Harper & Row, New York, 1968); *On the way to language*, trans. Peter D. Herz (Harper & Row, New York, 1971); *Poetry, language, thought*, trans. Albert Hofstadter (Harper & Row, New York, 1971) and *The question concerning technology and other essays*, trans. William Lovitt (Harper & Row, New York, 1977).

7. *Poetry, language, thought*, p. 86.

8. For the implications of 'post-metaphysical' see 'The word of Nietzsche' in *The question concerning technology*, pp. 53–112. For the recovery of pre-Socratic thinking see *What is called thinking*, esp. lectures V to X.

9. *On the way to language*, p. 22.

10. But see Raymond Williams's discussion of this poem in *The country and the city* (Chatto & Windus, London, 1973), pp. 27–34. Williams's demystification of the power relations in the poem gives a quite different emphasis to the construction of a world. A critical reading of the poem should accommodate these recognitions. To dwell within the poem is not necessarily to do so uncritically. Such an awareness, I would say, is more evident in Leavis than in Heidegger.

11. 'The nature of language' in *On the way to language*, p. 98.

12. Cf. *Revaluation*, p. 216, and the more sustained discussion in 'Imagery and movement', reprinted in *The living principle*, esp. pp. 110–12.

13. *Lives of the English poets*, ed. G. Birkbeck Hill (Oxford University Press, London, 1905), vol. III, pp. 230–2.

14. 'Epistle to Dr Arbuthnot', lines 163–4.

15. 'The enactment fallacy', *Essays in Criticism, XXX* (April 1980), 95–104.

16. As, for example: 'The curious inertness continues to prevail — a

fact that comes home to the reader who is in the habit of feeling his way to the proper reading out of poetry he takes seriously: there seems to be no life here to the rhythm and tone', *The living principle*, p. 254.

17. 'The way to language' in *The way to language*, p. 133.

18. 'Language' in *Poetry, language, thought*, p. 208.

19. Raymond Williams, *The long revolution* (Chatto & Windus, London, 1961) p. 45.

20. Part of this essay is in *The portable Nietzsche*, ed. and trans. Walter Kaufmann (Viking Press, New York, 1954), pp. 42–7.

21. Trans. Robert Czerny *et al.* (Routledge & Kegan Paul, London, 1978). Originally *La Métaphore vive* (Paris, 1975).

22. *Twilight of the idols*, 'The problem of Socrates', esp. sections 8–12.

23. See, for example, his comments on Wordsworth's 'thinking' in *Revaluation*, pp. 130–7.

Chapter 5

1. Although Leavis disapproved of this phrase. Cf. *The living principle*, p. 215.

2. *Selected essays* (Faber & Faber, London, 1932), esp. pp. 287–90.

3. 'In defence of Milton', *Scrutiny, VII* (1938), 1, 104–14.

4. Eliot later acknowledged this. See, for example, his remarks on Donne in 'Lancelot Andrewes', *Selected essays*, pp. 341–53, and his 1947 lecture on 'Milton', reprinted in *On poetry and poets* (Faber & Faber, London, 1943), p. 173.

5. *Essays in critical dissent* (Longman, London, 1972), pp. 142–52.

6. *English literature in our time and the university*, pp. 85–6.

7. See also the exchange between F. W. Bateson and Leavis in which Leavis argued the primacy of critical judgement in constituting the 'historical material'. Leavis reviewed Bateson's *English poetry and the English language* in *Scrutiny, IV* (1935), 1, 96–100. Bateson replied, in *IV* (1935), 2, 181–5. Their more sustained exchange was in Bateson's 'The function of criticism at the present time', *Essays in Criticism, III* (1953), 1, 1–27, and Leavis's 'The responsible critic: or the function of criticism at any time', *Scrutiny, XIX* (1953), 3, 162–83.

8. *Lectures in America*, pp. 59–81. Although the comparison of 'Byzantium' and 'Sailing to Byzantium' had been published earlier.

9. *English literature in our time and the university*, pp. 136–7.

10. *The survival of English* (Cambridge University Press, Cambridge, 1973), p. 39.

11. P. J. M. Robertson, *The Leavises on fiction: an historic partnership* (Macmillan, London, 1981), p. 42, has noted I. A. Richards's formulation: 'to say we are impersonal is merely a curious way of saying that our personality is more completely involved'. The quizzical obliqueness of this suggests none the less a difference between the spirit of his recognition and Leavis's as is noted in *The common pursuit*, p. 134. The fullest discussion of the whole issue of 'impersonality' is in Vincent Buckley, *Poetry and morality:*

studies in the criticism of Matthew Arnold, T. S. Eliot and F. R. Leavis (Chatto & ·Windus, London,˙ 1959).

12. For a close reading of Eliot's essay see Brian Lee, *Theory and personality* (Athlone Press, London, 1979). There is a summary discussion in Robert Boyers, *F. R. Leavis. Judgement and the discipline of thought* (University of Missouri Press, Columbia, Mo., 1978), pp. 61–7.

13. For a detailed account of this, see Bernard Bergonzi 'Leavis and Eliot: the long road to rejection', *Critical Quarterly* (1984), 26, 21–43. I differ from Bergonzi, and most of the critics he quotes, in seeing Leavis as essentially right about Eliot, and the final essays on *Four quartets* in *The living principle* as corrective rather than dismissive. For Leavis, Eliot is the one modern poet who merits such sustained, almost obsessive, attention.

14. *Sincerity and authenticity* (Oxford University Press, London, 1972).

15. 'The Muse of Satire', *The Yale Review, XLI* (1951), 80–92. Reprinted in *Satire: modern essays in criticism*, ed. R. Paulson (Prentice-Hall, Englewood Cliffs, NJ, 1971), pp. 190–201.

16. See Leavis's comments on Pope's pun on 'port'. *Revaluation*, p. 84.

17. *English literature in our time and the university*, p. 114. See also Leavis's remarks on Pope's lines 'Ask not what Provocation I have had?/The Strong Antipathy of Good to Bad': 'We may not accept this as suggesting adequately the moral basis of Pope's satire, but it is significant that Pope could offer such an account: his strength as a satirist was that he lived in an age when such an account could be offered.' *Revaluation*, p. 74.

18. The phrase occurs in *The living principle*, p. 173.

19. *Exploration* (Macmillan, London, 1962), p. 305.

20. *The aims of interpretation* (University of Chicago Press, Chicago, 1976), pp. 4–5.

21. For example 'The Dunciad', *Scrutiny, XII* (1944), 1, 75.

22. Cf. L. C. Knights's review of *A preface to 'Paradise Lost'*, *Scrutiny, XI* (1942), 2, 146–8.

Chapter 6

1. *The great tradition*, p. 91.

2. I have developed this general point in *The sentiment of reality* (Allen & Unwin, London, 1982), pp. 15–39.

3. *F. R. Leavis* (Longman, London, 1978), p. 40. P. J. M. Robertson, *The Leavises on fiction: an historic partnership* (Macmillan, London, 1981), p. 28, makes a similar point.

4. A further aspect of Leavis's change of view on Dickens is the way his qualified approval in reviewing *The wound and the bow*, *Scrutiny, XI* (1944), 1, 72–3, became dismissal in *Dickens the novelist*.

5. *'Anna Karenina' and other essays*, pp. 92–110.

6. *The rule of metaphor*, trans. Robert Czerny *et al.* (Routledge & Kegan Paul, London, 1978), p. 285.

7. See Leavis's comments on James's symbolism as compared to George Eliot's, *The great tradition*, p. 116.

8. 'Leslie Stephen: Cambridge critic', *Scrutiny, VII* (1939), 4, 413–14.

9. Another objection sometimes made to terms such as 'subtle' and 'complex' is their exclusiveness; that only those possessed of an appropriate sensibility can understand. I believe this is wrong-headed. Indeed, it is a general truth well embodied in Leavis that a teacher should insist on giving the best possible understanding of a subject. That is the most truly democratic conception.

10. Actually Leavis is seeking something very like the Heideggerian 'world'.

11. Denys Thompson (ed.), *The Leavises: recollections and impressions* (Cambridge University Press, Cambridge, 1984), p. 92.

12. 'Components of the national culture', *New Left Review, 50* (1968), p. 50.

13. *Selected essays* (Faber & Faber, London, 1932), p. 16.

14. See also Donald Davie, 'Second thoughts: F. R. Leavis's *How to teach reading*', *Essays in Criticism, VII*, 3 (July 1957), 231–41.

15. The terms are from de Saussure, *Cours de linguistique générale* (Geneva, 1916).

16. For an indication of what this means compare the King James Version of the Bible with its modern replacement. See also Ian Robinson's discussion of the two versions in *The survival of English* (Cambridge University Press, Cambridge, 1973). Is it an indication of the effective invisibility of language in our culture that the arguments for the new version have not been advanced for replacing the medieval cathedrals with modern, up-to-date structures?

17. *Culture and society* (Chatto & Windus, London, 1958), pp. 246–57 and also the early chapters of *The country and the city* (Chatto & Windus, London, 1973).

18. *Nor shall my sword*, p. 85. Leavis denies the nostalgia but not the historical claim.

19. *Collected essays*, ed. G. Singh (Cambridge University Press, Cambridge, 1983–), vol. I.

20. Reprinted in *'Anna Karenina' and other essays*, pp. 33–48.

21. *London Review of Books, 8*, no. 17 (9 Oct. 1986), 22–3.

22. 'Dr Leavis, "English" and philosophy', *The Haltwhistle Quarterly*, no. 6 (Winter 1977), 1–13.

23. 'The use of "concreteness" as an evaluative term in F. R. Leavis's *The great tradition*', *British Journal of Aesthetics*, Jan. 1965, pp. 14–24.

24. Cf. John Newton, *'Scrutiny's* failure with Shakespeare', *The Cambridge Quarterly, I*, 2 (Spring, 1966), 144–77.

25. Ian Robinson has argued in an unpublished talk at the University of Warwick in 1985 that Leavis resisted a tragic vision of life. That might have a further bearing on Leavis's commitment to the novel rather than drama.

26. Leavis's essay 'Diabolic intellect and the noble hero' (*The common pursuit*, pp. 136–59) is a cogent refutation of 'sentimental' and 'scholarly' reductions of the play, but see John Bayley's discussion of the 'novel' in Shakespeare's plays with special reference to *Othello*, in *The uses of division* (Chatto & Windus, London, 1976), pp. 217–44.

Chapter 7

1. *The living principle*, p. 158.

2. Trans. Geoff Bennington and Brian Massumi (University of Minnesota Press, Minneapolis, Minn., 1984).

3. *Aesthetics, form and emotion*, ed. George Roberts (Duckworth, London, 1983), pp. 185–6.

4. Pole's final question about a passage from *Timon of Athens* could be answered by rereading Leavis's essay, 'Tragedy and the medium' (reprinted in *The common pursuit*), esp. p. 124.

5. For a negative instance, Kate Millett, *Sexual Politics*, (Doubleday, New York, 1970). For a positive example, on some of the same territory, Sheila Macleod, *Lawrence's men and women* (Heinemann, London, 1985). Only after coupling these names on their common theme did I note that Millett writes as a sociologist and Macleod as a novelist.

Select Bibliography

For detailed reference see D. F. Mackenzie and M. P. Allum, *F. R. Leavis. A checklist 1924–64* (Chatto & Windus, London, 1966) and the analytic bibliographies of Leavis's writings in Greenwood and Hayman (below).

Writing on Leavis

Anderson, Perry, 'Components of the national culture', *New Left Review*, 50 (May/June, 1968), 3–57. Covers a range of intellectual fields in Britain to argue a disabling lack of overall social theory. Concludes with Leavis's attempt to make literary criticism supply this 'absent centre'.

Bilan, R. P., *The literary criticism of F. R. Leavis* (Cambridge University Press, Cambridge, 1979). A close reading of Leavis, concentrating on the criticism of fiction, and countering many common misconceptions. Stresses the 'religious' dimension of Leavis.

: Boyers, Robert, *F. R. Leavis. Judgement and the discipline of thought* (University of Missouri Press, Columbia, Mo., 1978). Argues the unique coherence and force of Leavis's literary judgement while questioning particular instances. An intelligent reading although Leavis perhaps emerges as more wilful than the overall argument wishes to claim.

Buckley, Vincent, *Poetry and morality: studies in the criticism of Matthew Arnold, T. S. Eliot and F. R. Leavis* (Chatto & Windus, London, 1959). A comparative reading with good, extended treatment of 'impersonality'.

Casey, John, *The language of criticism* (Methuen, London, 1966). Considers a number of modern critics from a methodological point of view and concludes with Leavis's sophisticated blend of 'expressionist' and 'mimetic' principles.

Greenwood, Edward, *F .R. Leavis* (Longman, London, 1978). Brief but shrewd survey bringing out Leavis's 'sober Nietzscheanism' and his grasp of the essential in literary and cultural critique.

Hayman, Ronald, *F. R. Leavis* (Heinemann, London, 1976). Best introductory account indicating the historical and institutional contexts as well as the personal impact of Leavis's teaching. Covers all major topics in a personal assessment of the *œuvre* and includes a useful bibliography.

Inglis, Fred, *Radical earnestness* (Martin Robertson, Oxford, 1982). Traces a larger tradition of British cultural critique and elaborates the historical circumstances underlying it. The chapter on Leavis is a succinct defence of his intellectual, institutional and social postures.

Kaufman, R. J., 'F. R. Leavis: the morality of mind', *Critical Quarterly*, I,

145

3 (Autumn 1959), 247–52. An American view of Leavis focusing on the quality of the thinking enacted in his style. One of several symposiasts in this volume.

McCallum, Pamela, *Literature and method: towards a critique of I. A. Richards, T. S. Eliot and F. R. Leavis* (Gill and Macmillan Humanities Press, Dublin, 1983). Elaborates Perry Anderson's essential case. Some shrewd commentary on the theme of 'individual' v. 'society'. Early Leavis came close to defining 'alienated consciousness' but turned instead to a 'substantialist metaphor of organic growth'.

McLuhan, H. M., 'Poetic and rhetorical analysis: the case for Leavis against Richards and Empson', *Sewanee Review, LII* (April 1944), 266–76. Argues the greater complexity and sense of proportion in Leavis's critical judgements as opposed to merely rhetorical analysis. 'Rhetorical' here does not encompass the ideological and deconstructive concerns the term might now imply.

Mulhern, Francis, *The moment of 'Scrutiny'* (New Left Books, London, 1979). Fullest, most thorough account of Leavis through a critical history of *Scrutiny*. In recognising the force of Leavis's example, while remaining unable to assimilate him to his own radical premisses, Mulhern focuses a representative impasse.

· Robertson, P. J. M., *The Leavises on fiction: an historic partnership* (Macmillan, London, 1981). Argues the centrality of the Leavises' criticism of fiction in their joint *œuvre*. This may be true of their impact although the perceptions underlying it owe much to a 'poetic' understanding of language.

Steiner, George, 'Men and ideas: F. R. Leavis', *Encounter* (May 1962), reprinted in *Language and silence* (Faber & Faber, London, 1967), pp. 229–47. Concentrates particularly on the written style and personal manner of Leavis as an index of the man.

Strickland, Geoffrey, *Structuralism or criticism?* (Cambridge University Press, Cambridge, 1981). Takes Roland Barthes as a representative instance of contemporary forms of analysis which seek to displace critical activity as traditionally understood. Leavis's example is adduced to demonstrate the fallacy of this.

Thompson, Denys (ed.), *The Leavises: recollections and impressions* (Cambridge University Press, Cambridge, 1984). Mainly personal reminiscences but including several sustained critical reflections notably from Michael Black, John Harvey and David Holbrook.

· Walsh, William, *F. R. Leavis* (Chatto & Windus, London, 1980). Has a partly celebratory tone but includes some shrewd comments on Leavis's sense of language and his own use of it.

Watson, Gary, *The Leavises, the 'Social', and the left* (Bryn Mill Publishing Co., Swansea, 1977). A committed account of the Leavises' reception in Britain, partly for the record and partly to vindicate the broader Leavisian critique of British life.

F. R. Leavis: chronological list of principal publications
(published in London except where otherwise indicated)

1930   *Mass civilization and minority culture* (Cambridge University Press, Cambridge)

      D. H. Lawrence (Cambridge University Press, Cambridge)

1932   *New bearings in English Poetry* (Chatto & Windus)

      How to teach reading: a primer for Ezra Pound (Fraser)

1933   *For continuity*, ed. Leavis (Cambridge University Press, Cambridge)

      Culture and environment, ed. Leavis and Denys Thompson (Chatto & Windus)

      Towards standards of criticism, ed. Leavis with introduction (Wishart)

1934   *Determinations*, ed. Leavis with introduction (Chatto & Windus)

1936   *Revaluation: tradition and development in English poetry* (Chatto & Windus)

1943   *Education and the university: a sketch for an English School* (Chatto & Windus)

1948   *The great tradition: George Eliot, Henry James, Joseph Conrad* (Chatto & Windus)

1950   *Mill on Bentham and Coleridge*, with an introduction (Chatto & Windus)

1952   *The common pursuit* (Chatto & Windus)

      The complex fate by Marius Bewley. Introduction and two interpolations by Leavis (Chatto & Windus)

1955   *D. H. Lawrence: novelist* (Chatto & Windus)

1962   *Two cultures? The significance of C. P. Snow*, with an essay by Michael Yudkin on Snow's Rede Lecture of 1959 (Chatto & Windus)

1967   *'Anna Karenina' and other essays* (Chatto & Windus)

1969   *Lectures in America*, with Q. D. Leavis (Chatto & Windus)

      English literature in our time and the university. Originally the Clark Lectures delivered in 1967 (Chatto & Windus)

1970   *Dickens the novelist*, with Q. D. Leavis (Chatto & Windus)

1972   *Nor shall my sword: discourses on pluralism, compassion and social hope* (Chatto & Windus)

1974   *Letters in criticism*, ed. with introduction by John Tasker (Chatto & Windus)

1975   *The living principle: 'English' as a discipline of thought* (Chatto & Windus)

1976   *Thought, words and creativity: art and thought in Lawrence* (Chatto & Windus)

1982   *The critic as anti-philosopher: essays and papers by F. R. Leavis*, ed. G. Singh (Chatto & Windus)

1986   *'Valuation in criticism' and other essays*, ed. G. Singh (Cambridge University Press)

Index

148